DIVINE DAWNING
THE SAGA OF RAMAYANA
[A POETIC ODYSSEY OF LOVE, VIRTUE, AND VALOUR]

DR. DIPA MITRA

BLUEROSE PUBLISHERS
India | U.K.

Copyright © Dr. Dipa Mitra 2024

All rights reserved by author. No part of this publication may be reproduced, stored in a retrieval system or transmitted in any form or by any means, electronic, mechanical, photocopying, recording or otherwise, without the prior permission of the author. Although every precaution has been taken to verify the accuracy of the information contained herein, the publisher assume no responsibility for any errors or omissions. No liability is assumed for damages that may result from the use of information contained within.

BlueRose Publishers takes no responsibility for any damages, losses, or liabilities that may arise from the use or misuse of the information, products, or services provided in this publication.

For permissions requests or inquiries regarding this publication, please contact:

BLUEROSE PUBLISHERS
www.BlueRoseONE.com
info@bluerosepublishers.com
+91 8882 898 898
+4407342408967

ISBN: 978-93-5989-150-7

Cover design: Tahira
Typesetting: Tanya Raj Upadhyay

First Edition: February 2024

DEDICATION:

This book, "Divine Dawning: The Saga of Ramayana", is dedicated to all readers, especially those who are curious about ancient tales, but find traditional epics daunting. Through the power of poetry, this book offers a vibrant and condensed journey through the Ramayana, unlocking its timeless wisdom and relevance for the modern world. May it ignite your imagination and inspire you to discover the enduring magic of this epic saga.

PREFACE

"From Dawn to Eternity: The Saga of Ramayana" is a poetic odyssey that delves into the profound depths of one of the greatest epics ever told. This collection of poetry, spanning around 180 pages, embarks on a lyrical journey through the life and legacy of Lord Rama, weaving through the themes of divine love, virtue, and valour.

The book opens with "The Genesis of the Epic," presenting the birth of this celestial narrative and exploring Valmiki's quest to immortalize Rama's journey. "The Legacy of King Dasharatha" narrates the poignant story of Rama's father, capturing the essence of royal duty and the divine orchestrations that lead to Rama's incarnation. This section transitions into the heart of the epic with "The Divine Incarnations," detailing the celestial arrivals of Rama, his brothers, and Sita framing their destinies in the cosmic play.

As the reader progresses, they encounter "Divine Archery and the Swayamvara of Mithila," highlighting key moments like the breaking of Lord Shiva's bow and the fateful choosing of Sita. The subsequent chapters, "Celebration and Lamentation of Ayodhya" and "The Forest Saga: Clash of Fates," dive into the complex emotions of joy, betrayal, and the trials faced during the exile.

The narrative takes a dramatic turn with "Vanaras, The Forest-Dwelling Heroes and The Commotion of Lanka," where the valour of Hanuman and the anguish of Sita in confinement are poignantly depicted. This leads to the climactic "Confrontation of Rama and Ravana," a poetic representation of the ultimate battle between good and evil.

The next chapters, "Rama's Victory in Lanka: Echoes and Consequences" and "Uttar Kanda: The Odyssey Beyond," reflect on the aftermath of victory and the poignant tale of Rama and Sita's separation. The book culminates in "Rama's Voyage into the Infinite," portraying his divine departure and eternal legacy.

In "Unveiling Rama and Sita's Sacred Love," the poems delve into the depths of their divine relationship, exploring themes of love, sacrifice, and resilience. Finally, "The Contemporary Relevance of the Ramayana" connects the ancient epic's wisdom to modern life, offering timeless lessons in dharma, unity, and the pursuit of righteousness.

"From Dawn to Eternity: The Saga of Ramayana" is not just a book of poetry but a spiritual journey, inviting readers to experience the transformative power of one of the greatest stories ever told. Through its pages, the eternal saga of Rama is rekindled, offering insights and inspiration for the contemporary reader.

TABLE OF CONTENTS

THE GENESIS OF THE EPIC 1
The Journey of Rama: A Lyrical Odyssey 1

In Search of Virtue: Valmiki's Quest 3

The Grieve: A Cry for the Krouncha 5

The Birth of Poetry: Revelation 7

The Divine Mandate: Epic Charge 9

The Visionary Sage: Celestial Insight 11

THE LEGACY OF KING DASHARATHA 13
The Saga of Dasharatha 13

The Tragic Tale 15

The Divine Offering 17

The Royal Harmony of Ayodhya 19

THE DIVINE INCARNATIONS 21
Rama: Celestial Arrival of the Seventh Avatar 21

Lakshmana: The Serpent King's Shadow 22

Bharata: The Noble Guardian of the Throne 23

Shatrughna :The Warrior of Celestial Justice 24

SITA :The Earth Daughter's Celestial Dawn 25

DIVINE ARCHERY AND THE SWAYAMVARA OF MITHILA 26
The Saga of the Divine Archers 26

- The Journey to Mithila's Fabled Swayamvar...............28
- The Loom of Destiny: Sita's Choice........................30

CELEBRATION AND LAMENTATION OF AYODHYA 32

- The Joyous Dawn in Ayodhya................................32
- The Shadow of Deceit: Ayodhya's Dark Hour 34
- The Dilemma of Promise: Ayodhya's Heartache..........36
- The Exodus of Hearts: Ayodhya's Sorrow...................38
- The Twilight of a King: The Mourning 40
- The Vow of Devotion: Bharata's Pledge......................42

THE FOREST SAGA: CLASH OF FATES.................44

- Disruption of Demons..44
- The Golden Deception: Prelude to Abduction.............46
- The Enchantment of the Golden Deer 48
- The Masquerade of Evil: Sita's Trial 50
- The Abduction 51
- The Echoes of Loss: Despair in the Forest 53
- The Quest for Sita: Through Shadows and Sorrow 55

VANARAS, THE FOREST-DWELLING HEROS AND THE SAGA OF LANKA 57

- The Pact in Kiskindha: A Bitter Victory......................57
- The Quest of Angada and Hanuman...........................59
- Uproar of Lanka..61
- Sita's Mourning in confinement 63

- Hanuman's Odyssey to Lanka 64
- Hanuman's Promise and the Flames of Retribution.....66
- The Heart of Forgiveness: Sita's Compassionate Grace 68
- The Saga of Ram Setu: A Bridge of Faith and Will 69

BIVISHAN KUMBHAKARNA AND INDRAJIT: THREE DEMONS OF MYTH..........................71

- Bivishan's Solemn Plea...............................71
- Bivishan's Welcome in Rama's Fold 73
- The Divine Invocation 74
- The Fall of Kumbhakarna 75
- Ravana's Lament 78
- Indrajit, Scion of Lanka 79
- Hanuman's Herculean Quest for Sanjeevani 81
- Gudakesh: The Vigil of Lakshmana....................82
- The Duel of Indrajit and Lakshmana..................84
- Indrajit's Last Stand..................................85
- Ravana's Grief for Indrajit............................87

CONFRONTATION OF RAMA AND RAVANA 88

- Ravana's Ill-Fated Valour.............................88
- The Chariots of Destiny: Rama versus Ravana............90
- The Duel of Destiny: Rama's Compassionate Might....92
- The Heavens of Fate : Rama's Righteous Battle 94

The Clash of Cosmic Powers: Rama's Enlightened Warfare 96

The Honourable Warrior: Rama's Triumph 98

RAMA'S VICTORY IN LANKA: ECHOES AND CONSEQUENCES 100

The Dawn of Righteousness.....................................100

The Joyous Liberation...102

The Trial and Triumph..104

The Bond of Brotherhood 106

Odyssey of Exile: Ram's Fourteen-Year Sojourn........108

The Coronation of Joy: Rama's Return to Ayodhya...110

The Bitter-sweet Farewell 112

UTTAR KANDA: THE ODYSSEY BEYOND 114

The Serene Realm and Sorrowful Exile......................114

Twin Sons: Sita's Lullaby 116

Luv and Kush: Blossoming Under Guru's Guidance..117

The Challenge of Destiny: The Ashwamedha and the Princes 119

The Encounter of Rama and His Sons........................121

The Valiant Young Hearts 122

The Ballad of Destiny: Luv and Kush's Revelation.....124

The Reunion of Hearts..126

The Test of Truth: Sita's Second Ordeal 127

The Earth's Embrace: Sita's Divine Ascent 129

Lament of Innocence: Grief-stricken Lava- Kusha.....130

RAMA'S VOYAGE INTO THE INFINITE............. 132

The Golden Epoch: Rama's Reign of Harmony 132

The Twilight of Destiny: Rama and Lakshmana's Sacrifice...133

Embark on the Celestial Voyage 135

The Divine Departure: Lord Rama's Journey to Eternity..137

UNVEILING RAMA AND SITA'S SACRED LOVE 138

Celestial Union: The Divine Love of Rama and Sita ..138

The Eternal Vows..140

The Crow and the Compassionate: A Tale of Love and Mercy...142

Love Unbound 143

Echoes of Separation: Rama's Lament for Sita 145

Tears of Malyavata Peaks: Rama's Silent Witness.....146

The Paragon of Virtues: Ram's Multifaceted Love 148

In Forests Deep: Sita's Unwavering Journey.............149

The Hour of Separation: The Moment of Despair 151

The Dual Role of Rama: Love and Duty....................152

Resilient Grace: Sita's Unyielding Love 153

The Unwavering Love of Rama 155

The Resilience of Sita: A Love Unyielding 156

THE CONTEMPORARY RELEVANCE OF THE RAMAYANA 157

- The Eternal Saga: Rama's Legacy 157
- Echoes of Dharma: The Timeless Wisdom 158
- The Lessons of Unity 160
- Berries of Devotion: Shabari's Timeless Offering 162
- Greatness of Mother Sumitra 164
- In Love's Divine Path 166
- A Journey to Divinity 168
- The Wisdom of Equanimity 170
- Triumph Over Tempest 172
- Celestial Kinship: 174
- The Timeless Ideal: Ram's Virtuous Saga 176
- Echoes of Eternity: Ramayana's Resonance: 177

DIVINE DAWNING:

THE SAGA OF RAMAYANA

[A POETIC ODYSSEY OF LOVE, VIRTUE, AND VALOUR]

THE GENESIS OF THE EPIC

The Journey of Rama: A Lyrical Odyssey

In ancient times, when whispers dance in Sanskrit grace,
There arose a tale from Valmiki's sacred space.
A story etched in time's eternal embrace,
The Ramayana, is an epic of celestial trace.

Behold the prince, Rama, of virtue and might,
Whose very essence, like the sun, shone bright.
Embarking on a journey, a path of righteous fight,
To reclaim his love, eclipsed by Ravana's night.

In forests deep, where shadows hold their sway,
Through trials and tempests, Rama made his way.
With Sita's love, his beacon, never led astray,
A testament to honour, in his heart, did stay.

Ravana, the demon king, in his darkened hall,
His power was immense, his pride before the fall.
But against Rama's valour, every fortress shall
Crumble, for good's triumph is destined to enthral.

The 'Ramayanam' is more than mere poetic lore,
A journey of a soul, through 'Ayanam's (life-story) core.
Through duty, honour, love, it opens a door,
To a world where dharma reigns forevermore.

So let this tale, in Sanskrit's beauty, be told,
Of Rama, the prince, so brave and bold.
In each verse, a lesson, a truth to unfold,
A timeless saga of good over evil, gold.

For in the heart of this celestial narrative,
Lies the essence of life, pure and illustrative.
The Ramayana, through ages, shall live,
A beacon of hope, in the tales we give.

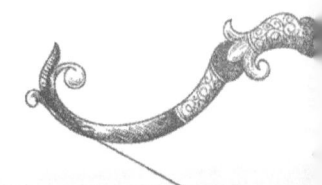

In Search of Virtue: Valmiki's Quest

In age-old groves, where wisdom's whispers play,
Sage Valmiki sought truths, his haven's sway.
To Narada, divine, his questions unfurled,
"Who personifies virtue, throughout the world?"

"Who in this world, stands alone so bright,
A paragon of principles, a beacon of light?
In deeds and words, unyieldingly upright,
A soul so pure, in the darkest night?"

"Who speaks the truth, unwavering, so bold,
Whose actions and thoughts can never be sold?
In the labyrinth of life, unswayed, uncontrolled,
A spirit steadfast, in virtues manifold?"

"Who walks in kindness, to all life benign?
Whose conduct merges as the stars align?
In the tapestry of existence, gracefully they entwine,
A harmonious blend, a divine design."

"Who, in skills and wisdom, stands unopposed,
In the arena of life, gracefully composed?
Whose presence like a lotus, amidst mud, arose,
A sight of serenity, in repose?"

"Who is brave, yet masters his fiery ire,
In the face of fear, his courage aspire?
A light unextinguished, an eternal fire,
Non-jealous, resplendent, rising higher?"

"Who, even Gods in the heavens revere,
When roused to war, his might they fear?
Yet in his heart, compassion so dear,
A warrior of peace, crystal clear?"

Thus Valmiki pondered, in the forest deep,
Questions sown, in wisdom to reap.
In the silence, answers began to seep,
Of virtue and valour, in a sacred heap.

For in his quest, Valmiki found,
Virtue's seed, in every ground.
In every heart, it can be crowned,
Where love and truth are profoundly bound.

The Grieve: A Cry for the Krouncha

In the realm of dharma, where truths intertwine,
Narada spoke of Rama, a soul divine.
"A king of virtue, in Ayodhya's line,
With qualities that in the stars align."

But Valmiki, in his heart, yearned for more,
A deeper understanding of the lore.
In quest of knowledge, to the river's shore,
He wandered, seeking wisdom's core.

There, by the water, a scene so grim,
A Krouncha bird (crane), life fading, limbs dim.
Its mate in mourning, a sorrowful hymn,
A song of loss, at the day's brim.

In that moment, Valmiki's heart did break,
Witnessing the cruelty life can make.
With righteous anger, his voice did quake,
Cursing the hunter, for compassion's sake.

"Oh, hunter, ill-fated, in your blind quest,
You've torn a soul from its loving nest.
With your arrow's flight, you've failed the test,
Of dharma's path, in which we're blessed.

For this act, your name shall eternally dwell,
In tales of sorrow, that generations will tell.
The bird you slew, in love it fell,
And with its fall, your fate did knell.

You've disrupted the harmony of life's song,
Where love and peace to this world belong.
In your pursuit, so terribly wrong,
You've unravelled a grief, deep and strong."

Thus, in his anguish, Valmiki cried,
For the innocent bird that unjustly died.
In his words, a truth, undenied,
That in the heart of dharma, compassion must abide.

From this sorrow, a seed was sown,
In Valmiki's heart, a purpose grown.
To tell the tale of Rama, widely known,
A story of virtue, in every tone.

In the lament of the krouncha, a tale began,
Of Rama, the virtuous, the noble man.
Through Valmiki's words, across the land,
A story of dharma, forever to stand.

The Birth of Poetry: Revelation

In the heart of the forest, where silence reigns,
A sage wandered, lost in thought's chains.
Valmiki, the seer, in nature's domains,
Heard a bird's cry, echoing its pains.

As the Krouncha (crane) wept for its love lost,
Its mournful melody bore a heavy cost.
In its rhythm, the sage's path was crossed,
Words flowed from him, in the air, they tossed.

Absent-minded, yet with a soulful tune,
His words matched the bird's sorrowful croon.
A verse emerged, under the sunlit noon,
A poetic marvel, a divine boon.

He stood, in awe of his unintended creation,
A line of beauty, an artful revelation.
Humanity's first poetic expression,
Beyond the Vedas, a new manifestation.

The Vedas, divine, in their sacred verse,
But this was different, a human's converse.
From a heart of empathy, emotions immerse,
In that moment, poetry broke its ancient curse.

Valmiki realized, in that fateful hour,
His words held a newfound power.
A human voice, like a blooming flower,
In poetry's garden, he built a tower.

From pain and love, beauty was born,
A new art form, in the world, was sworn.
No longer to the divine alone adorned,
But in human hearts, poetry was formed.

Thus, from a cry of a bird, forlorn,
A poet's journey was newly shorn.
Valmiki's verse, like a beacon in the morn,
Marked the dawn of poetry, human and reborn.

The Divine Mandate: Epic Charge

In the quietude of his sanctified abode,
Valmiki rested thoughts in repose.
When Brahma appeared, in splendour, he glowed,
A divine purpose, in his words, arose.

"Blessed sage," Brahma's voice did resonate,
"By my design, a destiny awaits.
The words you spoke, a poetic state,
To chronicle Rama is your fate."

"Your voice shall carry the tale of the just,
Rama, the wise, in whom the world trusts.
A saga of Gods and mortals, a must,
In metered verse, your duty thrust."

"Recount the adventures, the valorous deeds,
Of Rama and Lakshmana, in their heroic steeds.
The battles with demons, the sowing of seeds,
Of dharma and courage, in epic creeds."

"Speak of Vaidehi (Sita), her trials and plight,
Both known and hidden from mortal sight.
Every detail, in darkness and light,
Through your verses, shall be brought to height."

"Unknown stories, to you, shall be clear,
As if whispered by the cosmos, near your ear.
Your poem, a vessel of truth, sincere,
In its lines, the world's past and present appear."

"Your words, sage, shall never fall astray,
Truth in each syllable, in every lay.
As mountains stand and rivers sway,
So shall your Ramayana, forever stay."

"Your epic, a mirror of life's grand play,
In hearts and minds, it will eternally weigh.
A legacy of wisdom, in bright array,
Through ages and epochs, it will convey."

In awe, Valmiki accepted the divine decree,
A mission of verses, vast as the sea.
To narrate Rama's journey, in poetic glee,
A timeless story, for all humanity.

The Visionary Sage: Celestial Insight

In the hush of the hermitage, 'neath the sky's wide dome,
Valmiki sat, in meditation, his spiritual home.
Brahma's boon, a gift profound,
In the sage's mind, the universe's secrets are found.

A vision vast, a story untold,
The life of Rama, in his mind's eye, did unfold.
From Dasharatha's court, where tales are spun,
To the forests deep, under the setting sun.

He saw Rama, with virtue's light aglow,
Lakshmana by his side, facing friend and foe.
Sita, grace embodied, a spirit free,
Their lives are interwoven, like leaves on a tree.

Every smile, every sorrow, every silent tear,
Every word spoken, in Valmiki's heart did sear.
Through yogic power, a divine art,
He perceived their saga, every part.

Not just the past, in its storied might,
But futures unseen, came into his sight.
The joys and trials on destiny's path,
The triumphs and tribulations, and cosmic wrath.

In the sanctity of his ascetic grace,
Valmiki penned the epic's trace.
From Ayodhya's grandeur to the forest's embrace,
Each event, he captured, in time and space.

He wrote of battles, of love's fierce test,
Of dharma's journey, a relentless quest.
The Ramayana, in verses fine,
A celestial story, by design.

For in his lines, the truth did ring,
Of life, of Gods, of everything.
A cosmic play, on earthly stage,
Valmiki's epic, for every age.

His words, a river flowing deep and wide,
Through time's vast ocean, they shall forever glide.
The sage's vision, in poetic form,
In the hearts of the world, forever warm.

Thus, the Ramayana, a legacy divine,
Through Valmiki's insight, did it shine.
A testament to life's enduring song,
In the annals of time, it belongs.

THE LEGACY OF KING DASHARATHA

The Saga of Dasharatha

Before the dawn of Rama's eminent tale,
In the ancient scrolls, an epic prevails.
Of Dasharatha, king, a lineage divine,
An incarnation of Manu, in Brahma's line.

Born to Aja and Indumati's noble heart,
In Kosala's land, where heroes depart.
Nemi, his name, yet destiny had more,
Dasharatha, 'ten chariots', in lore.

His chariot, a marvel, across the skies it soared,
In ten directions, his mighty arrows roared.
With celestial speed, to earth, it returned,
In battle's heat, his valour brightly burned.

Upon his father's demise, the crown he bore,
In Kosala's realm, his legend grew more.
A warrior unmatched, his conquests wide,
Against Asuras' (demon) might, he stood, undenied.

Three queens, like jewels, adorned his throne,
Kausalya, Sumitra, Kaikeyi, their grace shone.
From Dakshina Kosala, Kashi, to Kekeya's sands,
They stood beside him, with love's eternal bands.

Kausalya, of serene light, a guiding star,
Sumitra, wisdom's vessel, from afar.
Kaikeyi, of fierce spirit, from Kekeya's wave,
In their union, the future's path they pave.

Thus begins the tale, in time's vast sea,
Of Dasharatha, the king, in destiny's decree.
A prelude to Rama's saga, under heaven's arch,
In the annals of time, his journey we embark.

The Tragic Tale

In the whispering woods by Sarayu's embrace,
Lay a tale of sorrow, a hunter's misplaced grace.
Dasharatha, prince of might, in shadows dim,
Sought his prey by sound, on a whim.

In the hush of dusk, a gurgle soft and low,
He loosed his arrow, swift as a crow.
A deer he sought, but fate had a cruel turn,
For a human cry did the silent forest churn!

Rushing forth, the prince, his heart in dread,
Found young Shravana, fallen, a crimson spread.
An arrow lodged deep, a tragic mistake,
A scene of sorrow by the quiet lake.

Mortified, the prince, his soul in despair,
Apologies fell, like leaves in autumn's air.
Shravana, young and forgiving, his fate he met,
A demand for water, his final sunset.

"Take this pitcher to my parents-blind,"
His voice, was a whisper, like a passing wind.
"They wait in thirst, for their son's return,"
In his last breath, a sorrowful sojourn.

The prince, now bearer of a woeful tale,
Approached the couple, frail and pale.
With heavy heart, he spoke of destiny's cruel hand,
Their son is a victim of an error unplanned.

Grief-stricken, the parents, in their world unseen,
Cursed the prince, in their agony keen.
"May you too know the pain of a child lost,
In the sea of time, by fate's tempest-tossed."

Thus, a prophecy of sorrow was born,
In the heart of a king, forever forlorn.
A tale of Dasharatha and Shravana's end,
In the annals of time, their stories blend.

The Divine Offering

In the age-old scrolls of Ayodhya's grand tale,
Stood Dasharatha, king, in hope's frail veil.
A dynasty's future, in silence, lay bare,
For a son, his kingdom's heir, he sought with care.

To the sacred rites to seek fertility, he turned,
For a progeny's blessing, his heart yearned.
Sumantra, wise, a prophecy he did reveal,
"Sage Rishyashringa's presence will seal the deal."

To Anga, the king ventured with hope's flame,
Where Romapada ruled, of noble fame.
His daughter Shanta, to the sage was wed,
To their abode, Dasharatha's footsteps led.

With Rishyashringa back to Kosala's land,
The Yagna ritual, was superb and grand.
Then followed the Putriya Isti, a sacred rite,
For sons, a prayer in the cosmic night.

From the holy fire, a figure emerged,
With celestial porridge, destinies converged.
"To your queens, this divine offering give,"
Spoke the being, "and through them, new lives shall live."

To Kausalya, Sumitra, and Kaikeyi fair,
The porridge was given, with utmost care.
A division sacred, in hope and trust,
A future was sown, from the cosmic dust.

From Kausalya, Rama, the Visnu, was born,
Kaikeyi brought Bharata, a new dawn.
Sumitra, bestowed with twins, like sweet melody-
Lakshmana and Shatrughna, the blessed rhapsody.

Thus, from Dasharatha's pious quest,
Came forth sons, among the best.
In the annals of time, their story shines,
A legacy of divinity, in the cosmic confines.

The Royal Harmony of Ayodhya

In Ayodhya's ancient and hallowed halls,
Where destiny's echo softly calls,
Reigned Dasharatha, king of noble fame,
His lineage a story, a royal flame.

Three queens graced his life, stars in his sky,
Kaushalya, Kaikeyi, Sumitra, by and by.
Each a pillar in the palace grand,
In their grace, the kingdom did stand.

Four sons, like jewels in the crown,
Rama, Lakshmana, Bharata, Shatrughana, renown.
Rama, the epitome of perfection's art,
A prince of virtue, pure of heart.

In the gardens of love and brotherly ties,
The four grew under the watchful skies.
Each unique, yet together so strong,
In unity, they righted wrong.

Rama, with his gentle, guiding hand,
A beacon of hope for the troubled land.
Lakshmana, his shadow, loyal and true,
A bond unbreakable, like morning dew.

Bharata, the embodiment of justice and care,
A prince whose qualities were beyond compare.
And Shatrughana, brave, a force unseen,
Together, they formed a team serene.

In the palace of Ayodhya, love was the theme,
A family, a unit, a singular dream.
In each brother, a reflection of the other,
In their hearts, the love of father and mother(s).

Thus, in Ayodhya, under the sun and moon's glow,
Four brothers lived, letting their affections show.
A tale of unity, in the sands of time sown,
In the royal harmony of Ayodhya, forever known.

THE DIVINE INCARNATIONS

Rama: Celestial Arrival of the Seventh Avatar

In the ancient tapestry of time, woven with cosmic strands,
Lies a tale of divine descent, in sacred lands.
Rama, the seventh avatar, Vishnu's incarnate grace,
A beacon of Dharma, in the human race.

"Delightful," his name whispers, "Charming" it sings,
A melody of righteousness, from heavenly strings.
His birth, a confluence of celestial omens bright,
In cosmic theatres, bathed in divine light.

Celestial lights danced, in a jubilant cosmic choir,
As celestial music echoed, transcending the higher.
Each star, a witness to this divine manifestation,
Each breeze was a carrier of his righteous proclamation.

In Rama, the balance of Dharma was gently restored,
In his being, the might of evil was forever deplored.
A symbol of virtue, in a world torn and riven,
Rama, the preserver, by the Gods, was given.

His arrival, a chapter in the eternal epic of time,
A verse of hope, in a world sublime.
Rama, a name etched in the annals of the divine,
A beacon of light, eternally destined to shine.

Lakshmana: The Serpent King's Shadow

In the celestial realms, where myths and legends entwine,
Lies a tale of devotion, as old as time.
Lakshmana, the loyal, Vishnu's serpent king reborn,
In human guise, with virtues adorned.

Beloved brother to Rama, his shadow, his might,
A presence is unwavering, in day and night.
The incarnation of Shesha, on cosmic waves tossed,
In Lakshmana, his essence, is never once lost.

"Marked by auspicious signs," his name doth declare,
A testament of fidelity, beyond compare.
In every step, in every breath of life's dance,
His devotion to Rama, more than mere chance.

Selfless sacrifice, his unspoken creed,
For Rama's cause, his soul pledged to bleed.
Protector, companion, in trials and strife,
His loyalty, is a beacon, in Rama's life.

In the echoes of epics, in the whispers of lore,
Lakshmana's legend, forevermore.
A symbol of dedication, in the mortal plane,
His story, is a melody in the cosmic refrain.

In the shadow of greatness, his light shines bright,
A star in the darkness, in the eternal night.
Lakshmana, the faithful, in history's grand tapestry,
A portrait of devotion, for eternity.

Bharata: The Noble Guardian of the Throne

In the annals of time, where legends are sown,
Stands Bharata, a figure of virtue well-known.
His tale, an epic of valour and might,
Echoes through ages, a beacon of light.

Associated with Indra, the celestial king,
His life a melody that the heavens sing.
In the realm of mortals, his role, divine,
A bearer of duty, in a royal line.

Though born to ascend to the coveted throne,
His humility shone like a gemstone.
Refusing the crown, a selfless deed,
To Rama's will, he paid heed.

"Nourished" his name, in depth and breadth,
Reflecting his essence, till his last breath.
A reservoir of compassion, deep and grand,
Guiding his people with a gentle hand.

In Bharata's spirit, a confluence of strength,
His capacity for understanding, at great length.
A beacon of hope, in turbulent seas,
A keeper of peace, in gentle breeze.

Through his story, a lesson unfolds,
Of virtues more precious than the purest gold's.
Bharata, the righteous, in history's grand weave,
A legacy of honour, forever to achieve.

Shatrughna : The Warrior of Celestial Justice

In the tapestry of lore, where divine sagas unfold,
Lies the tale of Shatrughna, brave and bold.
Lakshmana's twin brother, in shadows of unseen,
Yet in his essence, fierce and keen.

Embodiment of Yama, death and justice his creed,
In every action, every valiant deed.
A warrior in spirit, in heart, in name,
In the annals of time, he carves his fame.

In valour's embrace, his spirit adorned,
In battles and quests, his honour reborn.
With Bharata, a duo of strength and will,
Their foes' dark ambitions, they tirelessly still.

"Destroyer of enemies," his name doth resound,
In his presence, evil cannot abound.
A strategist, a thinker, in war's grand game,
Shatrughna, a force untamed, yet tame.

In the epic Ramayana, his role so vital,
A hero unsung, in challenges pivotal.
His loyalty to Rama, a beacon so bright,
Guiding through darkness, like a star in the night.

In his journey, a lesson of loyalty and might,
A reminder of justice, in the darkest plight.
Shatrughna, the youngest, in battle he stands,
A symbol of strength, in divine hands.

SITA : The Earth Daughter's Celestial Dawn

In the annals of time, where myths softly tread,
Lies the divine tale of Sita's earth-born bed.
In a field sacred, under the sun's watchful eye,
King Janaka ploughed, and the heavens did sigh.

From the furrowed earth, a miracle did spring,
In a golden chest, an unearthly offering.
Sita, the luminous, Bhumi's child so bright,
A beacon of purity, bathed in celestial light.

Daughter of the Earth, in a chest of gold,
A story of wonder, agelessly old.
Her emergence, a symbol of life's endless cycle,
In nature's bosom, a scriptural recital.

In the tapestry of legends, Sita's light,
Goddess Laxmi, pure and bright.
Daughter, wife, mother, ideals define,
Siyaram's (Sita and Ram) union is truly divine.

Through trials vast, her virtues stood,
Exemplary, life's sacred good.
A symbol of truth, in womanhood's embrace,
Love and virtue, Sita's grace.

In the tapestry of legends, Sita's tale is sewn,
A divine birth, in sacred scriptures known.
The Earth Daughter, from the land she rose,
In her, the heart of the cosmos gently glows.

DIVINE ARCHERY AND THE SWAYAMVARA OF MITHILA

The Saga of the Divine Archers

In lore's embrace, where tales unfold with grace,
Rama and Lakshman, in mythic echoes, find their place.
Summoned by sage Vishwamitra, a seer of great might,
To protect his ashram, and demons to fight.

From the royal abode of their father, Dasharath the wise,
They ventured forth, under the celestial skies.
Great archers of renown, with bows in hand,
Destined to defend the sacred land.

The Rakshasas, the demons of darkness and dread,
Lurked in shadows, their reign widespread.
But Rama and Lakshman, fearless and bold,
Faced the darkness, courageous and cold.

With arrows swift and true, they struck their foes,
Vanquishing evil, ending sorrows and woes.
Each demon fell, under their unerring aim,
Their valour and prowess, earning immortal fame.

The brothers, united in purpose and skill,
Fulfilled the sage's wish, with steadfast will.
The ashram, once besieged by terror and night,
Now bathed in peace, in the divine light.
In this ancient tale, a lesson is sown,

Of courage, duty, and strength shown.
Rama and Lakshman, in legend and song,
In the hearts of the faithful, forever belong.

So sings the bard, of the archers divine,
Whose deeds in the stars eternally shine.
Heroes of yore, in timeless glory cast,
In the saga of the divine archers, forever to last.

The Journey to Mithila's Fabled Swayamvar

Upon the remnants of battle, where silence fell,
A new tale arose, as if by a mystic spell.
Sage Vishwamitra, seer of ancient days,
Heard of Mithila's Swayamvar, set ablaze.

King Janak of Mithila, wise and fair,
Announced a contest, rare as the air.
For Sita, his daughter, a bride to seek,
A challenge for the brave, not for the meek.

With demons vanquished, and peace restored,
Viswamitra, with princes, towards Mithila soared.
Rama and Lakshman, brave of heart,
Joined this journey, a new chapter to start.

Towards the kingdom of Mithila, they tread,
With stories of valour and courage spread.
Leaving Ayodhya's realm, home of Dasharath the Great,
They ventured forth, embracing fate.

In their hearts, a fire of anticipation burned,
For Sita's hand, many a suitor yearned.
But in Rama's destiny, a secret thread was spun,
A tale of love and duty, not yet done.

So marched they on, under the sun's golden gaze,
Through forests and valleys, in a mystical haze.
To Mithila, where fate's dance would unfurl,
In the quest for the hand of the earth-born pearl.

In this journey, the seeds of epic tales were sown,
In the annals of time, forever to be known.
To Mithila's Swayamvar, with hope and might,
They journeyed, carrying the future's light.

The Loom of Destiny: Sita's Choice

In the realm where legends breathe and dance,
Stands Princess Sita, in her radiant glance.
Daughter of Janaka, in beauty and grace unbound,
Her Swayamvar, a quest where true love is found.

From kingdoms afar, where eagles dare to soar,
Came princes and kings, in lore and more.
Each eyeing the prize, in heart's fervent wish,
To win the hand of Sita, life's most precious bliss.

But this contest of hearts was no mere play of thrones,
It called for valour beyond muscles and bones.
A trial of skill, of spirit, of inner flame,
To fulfil a challenge, in Shiva's name.

The divine bow, Haradhanu, a celestial sight,
Lay in wait, a test of might.
To string this bow, no ordinary feat,
A task daunting, for the elite.

Sita, in her grace, watched with silent eyes,
As suitor after suitor met their demise.
Not in strength alone, but in heart's intent,
The bow would yield, to the right event.

Then came Rama, with a gentle stride,
In his gaze, the ocean's tide.
With unwavering hand and calm of the deep,
He approached the challenge, a mountain steep.

With a touch, a whisper, a harmonious link,
The bow succumbed, in a moment's blink.
In that instant, destiny's garland was strung,
As hearts of the gathered, in unison, sung.

Sita, with a garland of flowers in hand,
Chose Rama, as fate's eternal band.
In this Swayamvara, more than a husband she found,
A union of souls, in love profound.

Thus, in the annals of time, the story is cast,
Of Sita's choice, in love that forever will last.
A tale of beauty, grace, and destiny's power,
Bloomed in Mithila's most luminous hour.

CELEBRATION AND LAMENTATION OF AYODHYA

The Joyous Dawn in Ayodhya

In the golden age of lore and legend's light,
A tale unfolds under the celestial sight.
After the union of Rama and Sita, so divine,
Came a joyous chapter in the lineage line.

Lakshmana, Bharata, and Shatrughana, brave,
Joined in matrimony, a new journey to pave.
Each with a sister of Sita, in bonds of love,
Their weddings blessed by the stars above.

Back to Ayodhya, the procession did return,
In the hearts of the city, bright emotions burn.
King Dasharatha, with pride in his eyes,
Welcomed his sons under the auspicious skies.

With his three queens, joy unconfined,
In their sons' happiness, their hopes entwined.
Ayodhya rejoiced, in festivities drowned,
As the princes with their brides were crowned.

Then came the proclamation, grand and clear,
A decision the kingdom held so dear.
Rama, the virtuous, the pride of the land,
Would be the next king, by Dasharatha's hand.

The city of Ayodhya, in a euphoric swell,
Celebrated the news, in joy they dwell.
The palace echoed with laughter and song,
A future bright, where they all belong.

In this moment of triumph, love, and unity,
Ayodhya glimpsed its destiny's purity.
A time of peace, of prosperous reign,
In the joyous dawn, devoid of pain.

Thus, in the annals of time, the story is told,
Of a kingdom united, brave and bold.
In Ayodhya's streets, the tale is sung,
Of the day joyous bells of destiny rung.

The Shadow of Deceit: Ayodhya's Dark Hour

In the heart of Ayodhya, where joy once reigned,
A shadow crept, in malice unfeigned.
Manthara, Kaikeyi's maid, with a heart so sly,
Wove a web of deceit under the sky.

The news of Rama, the future king,
To her ears, did not joy bring.
In the quiet chambers of queen Kaikeyi's heart,
She planted seeds of discord, an evil art.

She whispered of forgotten promises, of boons untold,
Urging the queen to be bold.
To ask her husband, King Dasharatha, for her due,
A demand that would the kingdom's peace undo.

To send Rama to the forest, a banishment dire,
For fourteen years, to quench her ire.
And to crown Bharata, her own son,
As Ayodhya's king, her victory won.

Kaikeyi, once loving, once kind,
Found herself in a tumultuous bind.
Her love for Rama, pure and deep,
Against Manthara's words, a steep, dark leap.

But the maid's cunning, relentless and cold,
Moulded the queen, in her venomous hold.
A heart once warm, now turned to stone,
Asking for boons, in a chilling tone.

The tragedy thus began, a sorrowful start,
As Dasharatha's world fell apart.
The heartache, the tears, in Ayodhya's domain,
Marked the beginning of a lamentable reign.

In this dark hour, the tale takes a bend,
Of love and duty, and hearts to mend.
A tale of Ayodhya, in shadows cast,
In the shadow of deceit, a spell vast.

The Dilemma of Promise: Ayodhya's Heartache

In the hushed corridors of time, a story unfolds,
Of a promise made, and destinies it molds.
King Dasharatha, noble and just,
Faced Kaikeyi's demands, a heart-wrenching thrust.

Two boons she asked, with a treacherous heart,
Her words like arrows, tearing apart.
The first, to exile Rama, beloved and pure,
To the forest's shadows, for years fourteen to endure.

The second was Bharata's rise, a crown's solemn claim.
Ayodhya's heart weeps, in sorrow's deep frame.
For a son's ascent, a kingdom's tearful eyes,
Within these demands, a silent ache lies.

Dasharatha, struck by disbelief and pain,
His heart was torn, in a tormented chain.
Furious, and anguished, he refused to bend,
To such malicious will, he wouldn't lend.

But Rama, the dutiful, the epitome of grace,
Learned of the plight, in this tragic space.
With a heart so vast, and spirit so high,
He chose to honour the promise, under the sky.

To keep his father's word, unbroken, pure,
He embraced his fate, with intentions sure.
Grief-stricken, the king, and Ayodhya wept,
As Rama's promise, silently, he kept.

In his sacrifice, a lesson so profound,
In duty and honour, his actions were bound.
Thus, in the annals of history, this tale is told,
Of a promise, a dilemma, in a saga bold.

In the heart of Ayodhya, a pain so deep,
In the memories of time, forever to keep.
A saga of love, loss, and destiny's sweep,
In whispers of winds, their stories weep.

The Exodus of Hearts: Ayodhya's Sorrow

In Ayodhya's realm, where sorrow now lay,
A tale of heartache unfolds this day.
King Dasharatha, stricken and torn,
Fainted with grief, forlorn and forsworn.

Rama, the dutiful, prepared to depart,
Leaving behind a kingdom's broken heart.
Sita, his consort, in loyalty's glow,
Chose to follow, in his shadow.

Lakshmana too, steadfast and true,
Joined the journey, as sorrows grew.
Kaushalya and Sumitra, mothers in despair,
Wept for their sons, in anguish bare.

Urmila, Lakshmana's beloved bride,
Stood spellbound, her pain she couldn't hide.
How would she endure these years fourteen,
Without her love, in scenes unseen?

Bharata and Shatrughna, away from this plight,
Unaware of Ayodhya's sorrowful night.
As Rama, Lakshmana, and Sita took leave,
The kingdom's heart began to grieve.

The people of Ayodhya, in a mournful tide,
Followed their beloved, with eyes wide.
A procession of pain, of unspoken cries,
Under the watching, tearful skies.

The streets echoed with silent goodbyes,
As the royal trio crossed the threshold of ties.
A kingdom in shadow, a lament so deep,
In the annals of time, eternally to keep.

Thus the exodus of hearts, in history's weave,
A moment of parting, for those who grieve.
Ayodhya's sorrow, a river of tears,
In the saga of Rama, through the years.

The Twilight of a King: The Mourning

In the hallowed halls of Ayodhya's reign,
A tale of woe and heartache, a king's pain.
King Dasharatha, of noble heart and crown,
Succumbed to grief, in sorrow drowned.

Did he recall the grieving parents of Shravan Kumar,
Whose curse took flight in destiny's blur?
Dasharatha's last breath bore Rama's name,
A lament woven in sorrow's flame.

His spirit, heavy with unspoken words,
Fluttered away, like the flight of birds.
In the silence of his chambers, a king lay still,
Leaving behind a kingdom, a void to fill.

Meanwhile, Bharata and Shatrughna returned,
To a city in mourning, where incense burned.
Astonished, heartbroken by the tale they heard,
Their souls stirred by every pained word.

Furious at Kaikeyi, and Manthara's deceit,
Their wrath for the treachery, none could defeat.
Manthara, the instigator of Ayodhya's plight,
Faced retribution, in the kingdom's sight.

Bitten and scorned for her cruel act,
Her fate sealed by her malicious pact.
Ayodhya wept, in sorrow and rage,
A chapter of pain, on history's page.

The death of Dasharatha, a wound so deep,
Left the kingdom in tears, in grief to steep.
A king who loved, who ruled with grace,
Now a memory, in time's embrace.

In this tale of loss, of a kingdom's night,
Lies a story of love, of wrong and right.
Ayodhya's mourning, under the sky's vast arch,
In the twilight of a king, a sorrowful march.

The Vow of Devotion: Bharata's Pledge

In the shadowed aftermath of Ayodhya's loss,
Stood Bharata, determined to cross.
With haste, he journeyed to seek Rama's face,
Yearning to restore him to his rightful place.

Through forests deep and rivers wide,
Bharata sought his brother, with hope as his guide.
Upon finding Rama at Chitrakoot, his heart did plead,
For the return of the king, Ayodhya's need.

But Rama, steadfast in his father's decree,
Refused the crown, his destiny to flee.
Despite Bharata's tears, his heartfelt cry,
Rama's duty to exile, he could not deny.

Bharata wept, his sorrow like a child,
His pleas and entreaties, meek and mild.
Then, a request, both humble and wise,
To take Rama's sandals, a kingdom's prize.

To place them on the throne, a symbol of reign,
Till Rama's return, to relieve the pain.
A promise he made, to rule as a seer,
A servant of Rama, in reverence and fear.

Rama, moved by Bharata's love so vast,
Hugged him tightly, a bond to last.
With approval given, a brother's embrace,
Bharata departed, with solemn grace.

Back to Ayodhya, with a heavy heart,
He began his duty, his kingly part.
Rama's sandals, on the throne they sat,
A reminder of his vow, where his heart was at.

Shatrughna's shadow, a constant embrace,
Beside his brother, in every space.
As Lakshman to Rama, steadfast and near,
In unity's echo, bonds sincere.

Thus Bharata ruled, with a servant's hand,
Guarding Ayodhya, till Rama's return to the land.
His pledge of devotion, a tale of lore,
In the heart of Ayodhya, forevermore.

THE FOREST SAGA: CLASH OF FATES

Disruption of Demons

In the tranquil haven of the forest deep,
Where shadows whisper and ancient secrets keep,
The trio, Rama, Sita, and Lakshmana, dwelled,
In nature's embrace, their peace upheld.

But fate, ever twisting, spun a new thread,
As Surphanakha, the lady demon, her intrigue spread.
Enamoured by Rama, in her heart a flame,
She proposed to him, unaware of his fame.

Rama, the virtuous, showed his dear wife,
Sita, the centre of his life.
Undeterred, the demon turned to Lakshmana's side,
Her advances relentless, in arrogance and pride.

Her nagging incessant, a pestering storm,
Until Lakshmana's anger took form.
In defence of Sita, against the threat so near,
He wounded the demon, in her malicious leer.

Fleeing in fury, to her brothers Khara -Dushana she sped,
Demanding vengeance for the blood she bled.
Demon brothers enraged, with their army vast,
Marched to battle, their shadows cast.
But Rama and Lakshmana, in might and skill

Stood firm against the advancing ill.
With valour unmatched, in the forest's heart,
They fought, their arrows a deadly art.

Demons' army, vast as the ocean's tide,
Fell to their prowess, nowhere to hide.
Only one survived, to tell the tale,
Of the demon host's tragic, woeful fail.

In the forest saga, where destinies clash,
Good overcame evil, in a thunderous crash.
Rama and Lakshmana, protectors true,
In the heart of the wild, their legend grew.

The Golden Deception: Prelude to Abduction

In the aftermath of the battle's fiery tide,
A lone demon soldier took to flight.
To Lanka's isle, where oceans roar,
He sought Ravana, of demonic lore.

In his ears, he poured tales of defeat,
Of Surphanakha's woe, bitter and replete.
Ravana, mighty and vengeful king,
Heard the call for revenge, a sinister thing.

Decreed he then, a plan most vile,
To abduct Sita, with deceit and guile.
To teach the forest-dwellers, a lesson dire,
His heart started burning in a nefarious fire.

He summoned Marich, a demon of craft,
A master of illusion, fore and aft.
Marich transformed into a deer, golden and bright,
A creature of beauty, bathed in light.

In the tranquil forest, where Sita resided,
The golden deer pranced, its fate decided.
Sita, entranced by its shimmering grace,
Yearned for the creature, in that peaceful place.

Marich's deception, a lure so bold,
A part of Ravana's plan, wicked and cold.
A trap set in motion, under the sun,
The prelude to abduction, cunningly spun.

In this stage of lore, where shadows play,
A golden deception led hearts astray.
The stage was set, the actors in place,
For Ravana's plot, a dark embrace.

The Enchantment of the Golden Deer

In the dense of whispering forests (Panchavati) of yore,
Where destiny's threads intertwined and tore,
Marich, the demon, in his master's scheme,
Played the golden deer, a bewitching dream.

Sita, captivated by the creature's gleam,
Expressed a wish, like a flowing stream.
Rama, to fulfill his beloved's desire,
Ventured forth, his heart afire.

With bow in hand, through woods he chased,
The golden deer, its path laced.
Marich led him far, in a cunning dance,
In the deep forest, under destiny's trance.

At last, Rama's arrow found its mark,
Piercing the illusion, turning light to dark.
And as Marich fell, a spell he cast,
In Rama's voice, a cry so vast.

Sita, alarmed by the distressful call,
Felt her heart in a fearful thrall.
Lakshman, though reluctant, was sent to aid,
Leaving Sita alone, in the forest glade.

But before he departed, with concern so keen,
He drew a line, unseen and serene.
The Lakshman-rekha, a protective bound,
A magical barrier, deeply profound.

He implored Sita, with earnest plea,
"Cross not this line, for safety's decree."
In the heart of the woods, a tale unfolds,
Of enchantments, deceptions, and heroes bold.

The Masquerade of Evil: Sita's Trial

In the shadows of the forest, where secrets lie,
Came Ravana, deceit in his eye.
Disguised as a sage, humble and meek,
He approached Sita, her kindness to seek.

The Lakshman-rekha, a barrier so strong,
He could not cross, to where he didn't belong.
With raised voice, he feigned a beggar's plea,
Sita, compassionate, as kind as could be.

She stood behind the line, pure and true,
Offering alms, as the good do.
But Ravana, cunning, declined her grace,
Refusing charity, from that sacred space.

Sita, noble, not wanting to offend,
Stepped over the line, not to condescend.
In that moment, the disguise fell away,
Revealing Ravana, in his fearsome array.

His laughter, wild, echoed through the trees,
A chilling sound, on the forest's breeze.
Sita, betrayed by her own good heart,
Found herself in a tale, darkly apart.

Thus the masquerade of evil, under the sun,
Unravelled a plot, wickedly spun.
In the heart of the woods, a tale took form,
Of a princess pure, and a demon's storm.

The Abduction

In the dense embrace of the ancient wood,
Where once peace and innocence stood,
Ravana, through trickery and deceitful guise,
Lured Rama and Lakshman away with lies.

With Sita alone, the demon king's plan,
He seized the moment, his treachery began.
Abducted her swiftly, to Lanka his course,
On his chariot, with demonic force.

But in the sky, a guardian did soar,
Jatayu, the wise bird of ancient lore.
With wings widespread, a shadow cast,
He challenged Ravana, his allegiance vast.

In a valiant attempt to halt the crime,
Jatayu fought against the sands of time.
With beak and talon, courage and might,
He faced the demon king in aerial flight.

But Ravana, ruthless in his dark quest,
Struck the noble bird, a blow to its breast.
With wings now severed, Jatayu fell,
His efforts a heroic, tragic swell.

As Ravana fled to his island abode,
Jatayu lay wounded, on the forest road.
A tale of abduction, of valour and strife,
In the saga of Rama and Sita's life.

Thus, under the canopy of ancient trees,
Echoes the story of treacheries.
And Jatayu, noble in his final stand,
Became a legend, in the sacred land.

The Echoes of Loss: Despair in the Forest

In the realm where shadows blend with light,
A tale of despair, bereft of sight.
Lakshman, hastening to Rama's side,
Found him victorious, yet his heart did chide.

Marich, the demon, lay defeated and still,
His deception ended, by Rama's skill.
But joy was short, as Rama's gaze did turn,
To Sita, his heart, for whom he yearn.

Together they rushed, with dread in their hearts,
Back to their cottage, where their life starts.
But silence greeted, a void so stark,
In the grove where once sang the lark.

"Sita!" Rama called, his voice a desperate plea,
Echoing through the forest, where she used to be.
No answer came, just the whispering trees,
In their leafy murmurs, no solace nor ease.

Rama, the valiant, now broken and lost,
His love for Sita, the unbearable cost.
How could he breathe, live, or be,
Without his Sita, his soul's eternity?

Lakshmana stood by, his own heart in pain,
Watching his brother's sorrow, like unending rain.
Words of comfort he tried to impart,
But what solace for a shattered heart?

The forest, once a haven of peace and love,
Now a testament to the cruelty of the skies above.
In the echoes of loss, in the silence of dread,
Lingered the fears, unsaid, widespread.

Thus, in the depths of the forest, under the sky's dome,
Two brothers grappled with fate, far from home.
In their hearts, a void, dark and deep,
In the echoes of loss, where sorrows seep.

The Quest for Sita: Through Shadows and Sorrow

In the wilderness vast, under sun and star,
Roamed Rama and Lakshman, near and far.
Their hearts heavy, in a relentless quest,
For Sita, Rama's love, put to the test.

Through valleys deep and mountains high,
Their calls echoed, under the open sky.
But fortune seemed blind, and fate unkind,
No trace of Sita, could they find.

Then, in their path, a sight so grave,
Jatayu, the wise bird, noble and brave.
Severely wounded, at death's very door,
Holding a truth, in his heart's core.

With labored breath, he revealed the tale,
Of demon's deed, so ghastly and pale.
The king of demon, with his treacherous might,
Had stolen Sita, in the day's light.

Jatayu's words, like a piercing cry,
In their sorrow's thread, a tale did lie.
With gratitude and grief, they bid him farewell,
As he departed, under death's spell.

Now knowing the foe, but not the path,
They wandered, fuelled by love and wrath.
Endlessly roaming, in search of a way,
To catch the demon, where their hope lay.

In forests dense and rivers wide,
Their spirits searched, side by side.
A journey daunting, through shadows and sorrow,
In search of the dawn, a brighter morrow.

Thus, the brothers, in their relentless stride,
Sought their beloved, with hearts open wide.
In their quest for Sita, through loss and pain,
Their love's testament, forever to remain.

VANARAS, THE FOREST-DWELLING HEROS AND THE SAGA OF LANKA

The Pact in Kiskindha: A Bitter Victory

In the quest that through wild landscapes wound,
Came Rama and Lakshman, where fate was found.
In Kiskindha's realm, where monkey-men thrived,
Their journey paused, hope revived.

Sugriva, the exiled, in his kingdom's shade,
Met these divine brothers, his plight relayed.
A pact he proposed, with a heavy condition,
Seeking Rama's aid for his ambition.

His brother Bali, strong and unjust,
Ruled Kiskindha with iron lust.
Sugriva's plea, to Rama he brought,
For justice and aid, earnestly sought.

Rama, torn by duty and need,
Agreed to the deed, with heavy heart indeed.
In love's blind fervour for Sita's return,
He chose a path, ethically stern.

In stealth, he struck, from shadows dim,
A fatal arrow, for Bali's sin.
Sugriva, now king, his throne regained,
But in victory's wake, a curse remained.

Bali's wife, in grief and rage,
Cursed Rama's future, an ominous page.
That he, with Sita, would find no peace,
In love's reunion, no sweet release.

A bitter victory, in Kiskindha's land,
Forged in desperation, by Rama's hand.
The pact was sealed, the deed was done,
But the shadow of sorrow, could not be outrun.

Thus, in Kiskindha, where destinies cross,
A tale of sacrifice, gain, and loss.
In the epic journey, of love and strife,
Rama faced the complexities of life.

The Quest of Angada and Hanuman

In a tale as old as whispered time,
Sugriva's command, a quest sublime.
To the four corners of the earth, they roamed,
In search of Sita, far from home.

North, east, and west, they journeyed far,
Under sun and moon, beneath every star.
Yet, their efforts bore no fruit,
And heavy hearts began to take root.

But hope flickered in the southern trail,
Where Angada led, through hill and dale.
With Hanuman, whose courage never frail,
Their determination, they vowed, would not fail.

Then, from the skies, an aged vulture, wise,
Sampati, of sight keen and size.
Elder of Jatayu, of stories high,
Revealed the truth beneath the sky.

"Sita, the cherished, in Lanka's hold,
A tale of sorrow and bravery bold.
To the island fortress, over waters cold,
Your path lies yonder, be steadfast and bold."

With this knowledge, their spirits soared,
Their purpose renewed, their hope restored.
Towards Lanka, their journey poured,
Guided by words of the winged lord.

Thus, the southern band, with hearts ablaze,
Set forth on the path, through the ocean's haze.
In their quest, a story for all days,
Of bravery, of hope, and unwavering gaze.

Uproar of Lanka

In Lanka's realm, where shadows fall,
Ravana's grasp held Sita's thrall.
Amidst the Ashok grove's embrace,
A captive in a demon-guarded space.

In the shadowed glades of Ashok's bower,
Where blooms weep dew and time stands still,
There rests a maiden, pure as a flower,
Held by a force of tyrant's will.

Lanka's heart, in turmoil, beats uneasy,
As Sita sighs beneath the ancient trees.
Ravan, whose thoughts once noble, now sleazy,
Holds her captive, blind to her pleas.

Guarded by demons, in whispered tales,
Her grace outshines their grizzled guise.
In those woods, where light softly pales,
Echo her sorrows, her silent cries.

Mandodari, queen of a troubled throne,
Pleads for mercy, for reason's reign.
"Return her, husband, let your heart be known,
For in this act, no glory you gain."

But Ravan, in his vengeful pride,
Turns deaf to the counsel of his bride.
Haunted by the insult, the hurt inside,
From those forest-dwellers, his rage won't subside.

"For Surpanakha, my sister's plight,
I shall avenge, in day or night.
No wise man's counsel shall set it right,
For in my heart burns an endless fight."

Thus Lanka weeps, in a silent moan,
As its king sits, unyielding, on his throne.
In Ashok's forest, where sorrow is sown,
Waits Sita, forsaken, sadly alone.

Sita's Mourning in confinement

In the depths of Ashok's shadowed grove,
Amidst the rakshasi's relentless stare,
There dwells a heart, once brimming with love,
Now drowned in the depths of despair.

Sita, the epitome of grace and sorrow,
Whispers her beloved's name with each tear,
Yearning for the past, dreading the morrow,
In a world where hope seems austere.

Her thoughts, like golden leaves in autumn's play,
Drift back to days of joy, so bright and brief.
Those times with Ram, where love held sway,
Now lost, leaving her soul in grief.

Each tear, a silent testament to her plight,
Each sigh, a remembrance of love's sweet might.
In the cruel grasp of the night's cold bite,
She mourns the loss of their shared light.

"Oh, Ram," she weeps, "my heart's sole king,
In your arms, life was a splendid spring.
Now, amidst demons, my sorrow clings,
To memories of our love's undying wing."

Thus, in her captivity, she remains,
Bound by sorrow's unyielding chains.
Yet, even in her deepest pains,
The love for Ram in her heart sustains.

Hanuman's Odyssey to Lanka

In the annals of myth, a tale so grand,
Of Hanuman's leap to Ravana's land.
Assuming a form, both vast and high,
He vaulted the skies, 'cross the ocean's sigh.

His journey, a saga of challenges fierce,
Where mythical beings his path did pierce.
A Gandharva Kanya, in demon guise,
Tested his mettle, his strength and size.

Mainaka, the mountain, rose from the sea,
Offering respite, a moment to be free.
But Hanuman, with time pressing near,
Refused the rest, his mission clear.

Upon reaching Lanka, a guardian bold,
Lanka Devi, the Goddess of Lanka, her story untold.
A battle ensued, fierce and fast,
As Hanuman's strength was unsurpassed.

In her defeat, Lanka Devi saw,
The prophecy's truth, without a flaw.
Lanka's end was drawing nigh,
As foretold by Gods, in the sky.

In the heart of Lanka, under cover of night,
Hanuman searched with keenest sight.
Through palaces grand and gardens deep,
He spied on Ravana, in his keep.

At last, in Ashoka's somber grove,
He found Sita, the embodiment of love.
Beset by rakshasis, and Ravana's leer,
Her resolve stood strong, despite her fear.

Thus, Hanuman, brave and wise,
Brought hope to Sita, under foreign skies.
In this odyssey of courage and might,
Lay tales of valour, burning bright.

Hence, in her heart, a flame burned bright,
Resilience wrapped in silent might.
For even in the darkest hour's plight,
Hope whispered of freedom's light.

Hanuman's Promise and the Flames of Retribution

In Lanka's heart, 'neath a sorrowed moon,
Hanuman stood, a boon so soon.
To Sita, in despair and gloom,
He brought a sign, a hopeful tune.

Rama's ring, in his hand he bore,
A symbol of love, of legends of yore.
"Mother, fear not, for Rama's core
Burns bright for you, forevermore."

But Sita, with dignity and grace,
Refused the escape, in that dark place.
"Not by another's hand," she said with face
Set firm, "Rama must avenge this base."

"Only he shall rewrite our fate,
And lift this shadow, this heavy weight.
For in his triumph, the story great,
Of Ramayana, we must create."

In Sita's gaze, Hanuman shines,
Worthy soul of sacred lines.
Nine Nidhis, gifts divine,
To Hanuman, a sacred sign.

Nav (nine) Nidhi's symbols, fortune's lore,
Hanuman's grace, forevermore.
In Sita's trust, a sacred bestow,
A tale of treasures, in verses aglow.

She handed him a token (decorative hair clip) dear,
To show Rama, her life, to cheer.
Hanuman vowed, with heart sincere,
To carry her message, without fear.

Yet, before his leave, with a fiery zest,
He vowed to Lanka, he'd be no idle guest.
Through Naulakha Bagh, his wrath expressed,
Toppling trees, in a vengeful quest.

In Ravana's court, bound and grim,
Hanuman's spirit, never dim.
With fiery tail, and a vigour slim,
He escaped, setting fire, on a whim.

From roof to roof, the flames he spread,
A beacon of chaos, of terror and dread.
With a leap of faith, from the fire-bed,
Back to Rama, his message led.

To Kishkindha, the news he brought,
Of Sita's plight, and the battle sought.
A tale of courage, a lesson taught,
In the annals of time, forever caught.

The Heart of Forgiveness: Sita's Compassionate Grace

In the depths of Lanka, where shadows danced,
Stood Sita, her spirit untouched, unburned.
Her heart, a bastion of forgiveness and light,
Shone through the darkness, dispelling the night.

When Hanuman, the valiant, offered reprise,
To vanquish her guards, their end to devise,
Sita, with a heart so forgiving and kind,
Pardoned their actions, their fates intertwined.

She saw beyond their deeds, coerced and dire,
A reflection of Ravana's unquenchable fire.
Her empathy, a river flowing deep and wide,
Saw souls adrift in a tyrannical tide.

Generosity, too, was her nature's song,
A trait that to her, did truly belong.
To Hanuman, she parted with her gem,
A gesture of thanks, a regal diadem.

In every act of kindness, every forgiving smile,
Sita's grace echoed, transcending every mile.
A lesson in compassion, in humanity's embrace,
A tale of resilience, dignity, and grace.

The Saga of Ram Setu: A Bridge of Faith and Will

In the epoch where myths weave into reality's hue,
A vast ocean lay, a challenge to subdue.
To Lanka's distant shores, a path unseen,
Lay hidden in the deep, a gulf serene.

Lord Ram, in reverence, sought Varuna's aid,
To calm the sea's wrath, a request humbly laid.
But silence reigned, from the ocean's throne,
Prompting Ram's arrows, through waters unknown.

The sea receded, revealing its hidden core,
As Varuna emerged, from the ocean's floor.
With regret in voice, yet wisdom in his plea,
Offered a path forward, a way through the sea.

"Seek Nal," he urged, "blessed by divine hand,
With skills unmatched, to bridge sea and land."
Nal, son of Vishwakarma, in architecture versed,
Destined to conquer the ocean's endless thirst.

With Monkey-force's strength, and Nal's guiding light,
A 30-mile bridge arose, a marvel in sight.
In just five days, through toil and skill,
A path was laid, by sheer force of will.

Yet, in tales sung by Tulsidas' pen,
Neel, Nal's twin, joins the legend's den.
Together, they crafted the mighty Ram Setu's span,
A testament to unity, amongst God, monkey and man.

A bridge of stones, floating on waves of belief,
Linking two worlds, in time so brief.
A symbol of hope, where despair once lay,
A testament to faith that guides our way.

In this story, where divine and mortal blend,
Lies a lesson of perseverance, without end.
The Ram Setu, more than stones and tide,
A bridge of resolve, where faith and courage reside.

BIVISHAN KUMBHAKARNA AND INDRAJIT: THREE DEMONS OF MYTH

Bivishan's Solemn Plea

In the halls of Lanka, grand and vast,
Stood Bivishan, noble and kind,
A voice of reason, amidst the tempest cast,
A light of wisdom, in darkness confined.

He spoke to Ravan, his brother, his king,
With words as gentle as a dove's wing,
"Cease this folly, this unworthy thing,
For against a divine power, you cannot win."

Bivishan, learned, of heart so pure,
Saw the truth, clear and sure,
"Ram, the avatar, his intentions secure,
To confront him, is to invite a downfall obscure."

"Return Sita, with honour, let peace reign,
In this act, there's naught to lose, much to gain.
For in war with the divine, all efforts are in vain,
And only sorrow will be our claim."

But Ravan, in his pride, blinded and fierce,
Scorned the counsel, words that pierce.
With a heart so rigid, none could breach,

Cast aside his brother, with a contemptuous sneer.
In ignominy, Bivishan stood,
His wisdom spurned, misunderstood.
Yet, his heart, steadfast and good,
Knew the path of righteousness, as he should.

Bivishan's Welcome in Rama's Fold

In the saga of strife and celestial might,
Stood Bivishan, a figure of wisdom and light.
Cast out by kin, in a moment so stark,
He sought refuge in Rama, a hope in the dark.

Distrust brewed in the hearts of many,
For a kin of the foe, suspicions aplenty.
But Rama, with insight clear and bright,
Saw the sage within, shining with light.

In an embrace, profound and true,
Rama welcomed the exile anew.
"For in your heart, wisdom resides,
And your counsel, in this war, shall be our guide."

Amidst the wary, amidst the unsure,
Rama's faith stood firm and pure.
In Bivishan, a heart so rare,
A soul of virtue, beyond compare.

Thus, in the camp where heroes dwell,
Bivishan's story, they'd come to tell.
A testament to trust, a bond so well,
In the battle's tide, a pivotal swell.

The Divine Invocation

In epic tales where myths entwine,
Rama's quest, a divine design.
Before the sea, to Lanka's line,
Sought Durga's grace, a blessing fine.

Not in Valmiki's verse, but in Puranas' breath,
Rama's worship of Durga, before Lanka's death.
A gesture of honour, in every step he saith,
To the guardian of Lanka, in faith's wreath.

Durga Devi, once Lanka's shield,
Before Ravana's reign, to her did yield.
Rama, a king, in battlefield,
To Durga's realm, his mission was revealed.

As a host, Rama stood, devout and pure,
Brahma as priest, the rite to ensure.
With lotus flowers, one hundred and eight, a lure,
To please 'Ma Durga', her grace to procure.

In this sacred act, a warrior's respect,
To the divine protector, none neglect.
Rama's homage, a subtle aspect,
Of a king's duty, to divine intersect.

Thus, Rama worshipped, with heart so bright,
Durga Devi, in her powerful might.
A king's etiquette, in heavenly sight,
Before crossing the ocean, into the fight.

The Fall of Kumbhakarna

In the land of Lanka, where demons reign,
Slept Kumbhakarna, in slumber's chain.
Six months awake, then six asleep,
His rest so deep, like oceans deep.

In Lanka's battle, intrigue takes flight,
Skilled soldiers sent, vanish from sight.
Ravana, desperate, schemes unfold,
To breach Rama's ranks, secrets untold.

In shadows, spies weave webs unseen,
Yet Rama's might remain serene.
A macabre ploy, a severed guise,
Rama's head, deception tries.

Sita, steadfast, denies the lie,
In love's truth, she would rely.
Ravana's plots, in darkness spun,
Against the light of love, undone.

Ravana, defeated, in fury's hold,
Called forth his brother, mighty and bold.
A host dispatched, to break his rest,
In a cave where he lay, in slumber's nest.

Like a mountain vast, in sleep's embrace,
Kumbhakarna's form, a giant's grace.
A feast prepared, a gargantuan spread,
To rouse the sleeper from his bed.

Deer and buffaloes, rice steaming hot,
Jars of blood, a fearsome lot.
He woke at last, a yawn so wide,
Devoured the feast, with hunger's tide.

The reason revealed, of his abrupt wake,
Ravana's plea, for his kingdom's sake.
Kumbhakarna advised, with wisdom's breath,
"Return Sita, and avoid death."

But Ravana's heart, set on revenge,
Stirred his brother, from wisdom's edge.
To duty and kingdom, his loyalty sworn,
To the battlefield, he was thus borne.

A demon in war, a force untamed,
Monkeys fell, their spirits maimed.
Even Hanuman, in his might,
Struggled against this fearsome sight.

He clashed with Sugriva, a battle fierce,
Through monkey ranks, he did pierce.
Yet, the monkey king, in valiant fight,
Wounded the giant, in his plight.

Then Rama stepped, with arrows keen,
Against Kumbhakarna, a sight unseen.
Arms, then legs, he severed clear,
Each fall, a hundred monkeys' fear.

At last, the fatal shaft did fly,
Struck his head, beneath the sky.
Kumbhakarna, in his final roar,
Crashed to the sea, to rise no more.

In his fall, a tale so grand,
Of loyalty, and a demon's stand.
In Lanka's saga, his name extends,
Kumbhakarna, the demon transcends.

Ravana's Lament

In the shadowed halls of Lanka's throne,
Ravana wept, in grief, alone.
The news of his brother's untimely fall,
Rang through the palace, a mournful call.

A titan fallen, a warrior great,
Kumbhakarna's fate, sealed by hate.
Ravana, in his sorrow's deep embrace,
Faced the loss, his heart's dark space.

Then Indrajit, son of fearsome might,
Stood before his father, a figure of light.
"Father, in your grief, do not sway,
For I shall rise in this fray."

With a promise of strength, a warrior's creed,
Indrajit vowed to avenge the deed.
To the battlefield, he set his course,
Bearing the weight of his father's remorse.

In his heart, the fires of war,
A son's duty, a legend's lore.
Against Rama and his valiant band,
Indrajit would make his stand.

Thus, from grief's ashes, a new hope rose,
A son's resolve, to face his foes.
In Lanka's saga, a chapter new,
Indrajit's strength, in battle true.

Indrajit, Scion of Lanka

In the realm of Gods and mortal men,
Stood Indrajit, of lion's den.
Elder son of Ravan, Lanka's crown,
Holder of prowess, of great renown.

Indraloka's (paradise) master, a warrior fierce,
His skills in battle, the heavens could pierce.
Armed with celestial weapons, a sight to behold,
In magic and sorcery, his power untold.

Once, when Ravana, his father, was held,
By Lord Indra (God-king), in bonds compelled,
Meghanada rose, in fury swelled,
Against the Gods, his wrath not quelled.

He struck at God-king and his elephant,
In a clash of titans, a cosmic spat.
Captured the lord of celestial seat,
A feat so daring, an exploit elite.

Back in Lanka, with Indra in chain,
A proposal of death, but in vain.
For Brahma intervened, with a plea so plain,
And Meghanada's heart, he did gain.

Refusing death, he sought a boon,
Immortality, a wish opportune.
Denied this fate, yet gifted anew,
A chariot celestial, in heavenly hue.

Brahma, impressed by the warrior's might,
Bestowed upon him a name, bright as light.
Indrajit, conqueror of Indra's realm,
In his title, a story overwhelm.

For fourteen years, sleep he must forsake,
To meet his end, a mortal's stake.
In tales of valour, in myths we partake,
Indrajit's legacy, forever awake.

Hanuman's Herculean Quest for Sanjeevani

In the annals of battle, in Lanka's fierce land,
The princes and warriors made their stand.
Through days of conflict, and nights unseen,
Unfolded the war, brutal and keen.

Indrajit, Ravana's son, in his wrathful might,
Struck Lakshmana down, with 'Shakti', in the fight.
A wound grievous, a dire plight,
Cast a shadow, over the light.

Then Hanuman, in his strength untold,
Took a form gigantic, brave and bold.
To Himalayas, through clouds rolled,
In search of the herb, as foretold.

Upon Mount Sanjeevani, his eyes did sweep,
Over herbs and flora, a verdant heap.
Yet, the cure elusive, in that mountain steep,
Left Hanuman in a quandary deep.

With a resolve as firm as earth's core,
He lifted the mountain, an incredible chore.
Back to Lanka, the whole he bore,
A feat of might, of legend and lore.

To Lakshmana's side, the mountain he brought,
A miracle of hope, with healing fraught.
In that act, a victory, not just in fight,
But of devotion's power, and love's pure light.

Gudakesh: The Vigil of Lakshmana

In the whispering depths of an ancient lore,
Where faith and duty blend at core.
Lakshmana, steadfast in his sacred quest,
To guard Lord Rama, in tranquil forest's rest.

With Sita by side, in exile's shadowed glade,
Lakshman's resolve, a vigilant crusade.
Night's cloak unfurled, yet his eyes never fell,
In devotion's embrace, he broke sleep's spell.

To Nidra Devi, the Goddess of Sleep's realm,
Lakshman besought, a helm at life's helm.
"Grant me wakefulness, for their safety's sake,"
His plea, a sacrifice he chose to make.

Impressed by his loyalty, so rare and deep,
The Goddess conceded, but sleep must keep.
Urmila, his beloved, in love's silent oath,
Embraced his slumber, in unwavering troth.

Thus Lakshman, Gudakesh, the conqueror of night,
Stood unyielding, a guardian of light.
For only he, the sleeper's bane,
Could bring Meghnad, the demon, to his end's reign.

Meghnad, fierce, of celestial weaponry heir,
Wielding Brahmastra, Narayan-astra, in war's affair.
Pashupat-astra too, in his arsenal's might,
A formidable foe, in every rite.

Yet, amidst battle's roar and heaven's frown,
It was Lakshman's hand that brought him down.
For in his vigil, a power was bestowed,
Beyond mere weapons, a fate foretold.

In this tale of old, where myths still sing,
Of devotion, sacrifice, and the strength they bring.
Lies the legend of Lakshman, a warrior's heart,
A tale of victory, where duty plays its part.

In the dance of destiny, where heroes rise,
Lakshman's tale, a saga of the skies.
Gudakesh, the wakeful, in history's breath,
A symbol of endurance, in life and death.

The Duel of Indrajit and Lakshmana

In the throes of war's relentless rage,
A tale unfolds, from history's page.
Indrajit, in pursuit of invincible might,
Sought his deity's favor, in secret rite.

To the temple hidden, his steps he bent,
For a divine power, his intent.
But Bivishan, once kin, now foe,
To Rama revealed this impending woe.

In the sanctum, where peace should dwell,
Lakshmana and Bivishan, against the spell.
Indrajit, unarmed, yet fierce in fight,
Clashed with utensils, in a strange plight.

Indrajit's worship veiled in shadows of night,
Whispers of curses foretell the devotee's plight.
As Nikumvila devi witnessed the disrupted rite,
Immortality's pursuit caught in destiny's bite.

Cursing his uncle, a thread of time unwound,
Indrajit sensed fate's approaching sound.
In the weave of time, a foreboding decree,
The demon-prince's destiny, a chapter yet to be.

Indrajit's Last Stand

In the waning hours of his mortal tale,
Indrajit stood, both proud and pale.
Knowing well the hand of fate,
He bade farewell, at destiny's gate.

To parents dear, and wife so true,
His final words, like morning dew.
A warrior's goodbye, heartfelt and raw,
In the shadow of heaven's immutable law.

Back to the fray, with courage ablaze,
Against Lakshmana, his prowess to raise.
With warfare's art, and sorcery's maze,
He fought, a comet's dying blaze.

But Lakshmana, in his celestial might,
Was a force unstoppable, a beacon of light.
With Indrastra in hand, a strike so bright,
He felled Indrajit, ending his fight.

On the battlefield, a warrior's dance,
Indrajit's fury, his final chance.
Vanaras fell, in a tragic trance,
As he sought destiny's last advance.

Twice he bested Rama, the prince so dear,
And Lakshmana too, without a fear.
Yet in this tale, the truth is clear,
Adharma's path, the end is near.

Indrajit, Atimaharathi, a legend's breath,
In his fall, a lesson's depth.
Strength alone, a fleeting wraith,
If against dharma, it draws its sheath.

Though he fled, with cunning and speed,
His heart burned, with a vengeful need.
To punish the insult, his deity's creed,
In battle's fury, he vowed to proceed.

A clash titanic, under heaven's eye,
As Indrajit swore, "Bivishan shall die!"
But Lakshmana stood, resolute and high,
A protector, a warrior, under the sky.

With celestial weapons, fearsome and grand,
Brahmastra, Pashupata, were once in Indrajit's hand,
Vaishnavastra too, a trio so grand,
Unleashed upon Lakshmana, a final stand.

Yet destiny's weave, so intricate and fine,
Saw Lakshmana stand, in power divine.
In the heart of combat, where fates intertwine,
The duel of ages, a story's design.

In the clash of wills, where Gods might gaze,
Lay the end of Indrajit, in the battle's blaze.
A saga of valour, through time's long phase,
Echoes in eternity, in endless ways.

Ravana's Grief for Indrajit

In the heart of Lanka, where shadows fall,
Ravana stood, a titan tall.
The news of his son's grievous end,
Struck him deep, a wound to rend.

Upon the battlefield, his son lay slain,
A story ended, in sorrow's chain.
Ravana, the mighty, fell to the ground,
Lost in a grief, profound.

Time passed, as he lay in swoon,
Under the mournful, silent moon.
When sense returned, his heart did break,
With a father's pain, for his child's sake.

Tears flowed, like rivers in the night,
For Indrajit, his pride, his might.
"Oh, my son," he cried in pain,
"In your loss, my life is vain."

Beside himself, in agony deep,
Ravana's soul began to weep.
A lamentation, raw and wild,
For the loss of his beloved child.

In his palace, once filled with cheers,
Now echoed with a father's tears.
A titan, broken, by fate's cruel hand,
In the twilight of his once grand land.

CONFRONTATION OF RAMA AND RAVANA

Ravana's Ill-Fated Valour

Upon a tower, high and grand,
Stood Ravana, overlooking his land.
The battle raged, a fearsome sight,
His warriors lost, in the fading light.

In the carnage's wake, his anger grew,
A storm inside, fierce and true.
To the Gods, he prayed, his ritual due,
In armour clad, a heroic view.

Majestic, he seemed, in his regal might,
A king prepared for the final fight.
Yet beneath the facade, a faltering plight,
For the tide of war was not in his sight.

He called his chariot, with a solemn vow,
"By day's end, our fortune shall bow.
Be it mine or Rama's, fate shall allow,
This war shall end, here and now."

Though in armour, he shone like a fiery star,
His destiny was written, near and far.
Heroic in looks, but with a scar,
For valour true, was from him, ajar.

The story tells, in its mournful creed,
That bravado alone, does not a hero breed.
Ravana, in his spectacle, failed to lead,
For true heroism, is more than just deed.

His love for show, a tragic flaw,
A king who ruled, but with an awe.
In his final stand, the world saw,
A losing battle, against dharma's law.

So stands Ravana, a figure grand,
A lesson in life, hard and bland.
True heroism isn't in a mighty hand,
But in the heart's quiet, humble stand.

In the annals of time, his tale is told,
Of a king so bold, yet so cold.
In his last stand, history's fold,
A story of pride, age-old.

The Chariots of Destiny: Rama versus Ravana

In the epic's heart, where fates collide,
The Gods themselves could not abide.
To Rama's aid, they sent a guide,
Indra's chariot, in celestial pride.

Matali, the charioteer, of heavenly lore,
Brought a chariot, with powers galore.
From Indra, Brahma, Shiva, it bore,
A divine intervention in the war's core.

Rama, wary of deceit's dark play,
Questioned the gift from the heavens' sway.
But Hanuman and Lakshmana did allay,
The fears, urging him to seize the day.

Upon the chariot, Rama rose,
With weapons in hand, to face his foes.
Destiny's winds, now clearly blows,
In this divine chariot, his confidence grows.

Meanwhile, Ravana, in fury's bind,
Charged forth, with a clouded mind.
Ignoring omens of every kind,
His chariot raced, to fate resigned.

The battlefield, a grand stage set,
Where hero and villain in combat met.
Rama, composed, his course was bet,
Against Ravana, in anger's net.

Rama's calm, a stark contrast,
To Ravana's wrath, in shadows cast.
The latter's fate, in anger vast,
Seemed doomed, his lot, forever outcast.

Ravana, blind to destiny's sign,
Charged on, in his fatal line.
While Rama stood, serene, divine,
In the balance of fate, a thin, fine twine.

In this epic clash, the world did see,
The power of calm over fury's spree.
For in Rama's grace, and Ravana's decree,
Lay lessons of life, and its mystery.

As chariots danced, in war's loud drum,
The moment of truth had finally come.
A battle of wills, to which some succumb,
In the heart of the epic, its climax, hum.

Rama and Ravana, in their final bout,
One driven by faith, the other by doubt.
In this cosmic duel, all about,
The nature of destiny, was spelled out.

The Duel of Destiny: Rama's Compassionate Might

On the battlefield, where destinies entwine,
Rama paused, in a thought so divine.
"If Ravana's army falls, might he incline,
To change his heart, to a path benign?"

But Ravana, in his relentless chase,
Unmoved by mercy, set in his base.
He blew his conch, in defiant grace,
Challenging the cosmos, face to face.

From the universe, a divine reply,
Vishnu's conch, in the vast sky,
Echoed back, in a celestial cry,
Matali, charioteer, joined, Indra's conch did fly.

The battle commenced, a fearsome sight,
Ravana's arrows, in furious flight.
Yet Rama's arrows, in their righteous might,
Stopped them short, in mid-flight's plight.

Rama's approach, logical and clear,
Offering Ravana a chance, to hold life dear.
A testament to goodness, sincere,
Even to those, in hatred's sphere.

With bow and arrow, Rama stood,
A symbol of heroism, for the greater good.
His weapons, not just of wood,
But of dharma, as they should.

Rama, the hero, in his valiant role,
Seeking to heal, to mend, to console.
His compassion, a significant toll,
In the epic's tale, it plays a vital role.

Thus, in this clash, where arrows danced,
Rama's virtues, in each stance, enhanced.
Against Ravana's fury, he advanced,
In the duel of destiny, fate chanced.

In this poetic saga, so grand and old,
The story of Rama, heroically told.
Not just of battles, fierce and bold,
But of a heart of gold, never cold.

The Heavens of Fate : Rama's Righteous Battle

In the heavens' expanse, where fate's strings are spun,
Ravana beheld Rama, in Indra's chariot, shone.
A fury ignited, at the Gods' chosen one,
His arrows unleashed, in hatred's run.

Yet Rama, serene, in his divine might,
His arrows, a shield, in the ethereal fight.
Even with Ravana's arms, a formidable sight,
None could touch him, in his righteous light.

Ravana, in his hypocrisy's dark embrace,
Fought against a divinity he once did chase.
His strength, is no match for Rama's grace,
A battle of morals, in the cosmic space.

To the sky, Ravana steered, with a vengeful heart,
Rama followed his duty to impart.
Though Ravana struck, with his deadly art,
Rama's resolve never did depart.

Rama's army, from above, faced their doom,
Yet Rama's arrows, through the sky, did bloom.
Each advance of Ravana, they did consume,
In the celestial dance, a relentless gloom.

A sorrowful moment, as Rama's steeds fell,
Matali wounded, a tolling bell.
Rama paused, in grief's swell,
A moment of indecision, in the battle's shell.

Recovery came, with a divine sign,
An eagle perched, a symbol benign.
The Gods' favour, in that very line,
Rama's path, once more, did shine.

Round the world, their chariots flew,
A cosmic chase, in a sky so blue.
Back above Lanka, from the battle's view,
Rama's arrows, through Ravana's armour, they knew.

Rama's goodness, his introspective soul,
Afforded him time, to reassess his role.
Rewarded with signs, he reached his goal,
In his quest against evil, he played his part whole.

Thus, in the skies, a battle of ages,
A story of morals, in history's pages.
Rama's virtue, as the war rages,
A testament to dharma, through the epochs' stages.

The Clash of Cosmic Powers: Rama's Enlightened Warfare

In the vast arena of celestial strife,
Ravana wielded weapons, with fury rife.
A battle no longer of mere mortal life,
But of supernatural forces, sharp as a knife.

Rama, undaunted, his arrows so true,
Each armaments of Ravana, he calmly subdued.
Then came the illusion, a deceptive ruse,
Phantom armies, a spectral abuse.

Matali, now revived, with wisdom so rare,
Guided Rama to counter the spectral snare.
Invoking a weapon of insight, beyond compare,
The phantoms vanished, into thin air.

Ravana, in desperation, played his dark hand,
Summoning a storm, over sea and land.
But Rama, with a counter-attack, did stand,
Dispelling the chaos, with a gesture grand.

Then came the deadliest weapons of all,
An 'astra' against which, many would fall.
But Rama, in his calmness, did not stall,
With a mantra, he caused the weapon's downfall.

Ravana, in shock, his belief in a twist,
"Could Rama be divine, an avatar in our midst?"
Yet, in his rage, the truth he dismissed,
Resolved to fight, his fate to resist.

He hurled flaming weapons, a fiery tide,
But Rama, unflinching, turned them aside.
Back at Ravana, they were defied,
A reflection of his own anger, amplified.

Rama, a hero not just of physical might,
But of wisdom, perception, and a guiding light.
In the face of deception, he stood upright,
With divine knowledge, he fought the fight.

Ravana, though questioning, chose his path,
Blinded by fury, unable to grasp.
That destiny's logic, in his wrath,
Was leading him to an inevitable aftermath.

In this epic battle, where powers collide,
Rama's enlightenment, his truest guide.
A hero not just in battle, but inside,
Where wisdom and self-knowledge reside.

The Honourable Warrior: Rama's Triumph

In the tumult of war, where destinies clash,
Ravana stood, his hopes turned to ash.
While Rama, ever stronger, in his valorous dash,
Unleashed his arrows, in a thunderous flash.

Ravana's heads, severed in the fray,
Regrew anew, in a monstrous display.
Devils and demons in the chaos, did play,
Feasting on the fallen, in a grotesque ballet.

Yet, as Ravana faltered, and faintness took hold,
Rama, the honourable, in his attack he controlled.
In this moment of weakness, he did not unfold,
His strike, for honour, more precious than gold.

Ravana, revived, in anger, berated his steer,
Who revealed Rama's mercy, in the midst of fear.
Ravana, in this truth, saw something clear,
An honour in Rama, distinct and sincere.

With renewed fury, Ravana hurled his might,
Rama, poised, knew the time was right.
To end this war, in this last fight,
With a special 'astra' (weapon), with a divine light..

He prayed, invoking the astra's power,
Aimed at Ravana's heart, in the final hour.
For his arms and heads, though strong as a tower,
His heart remained vulnerable, a fatal flower.

The astra struck, with divine force,
Ravana fell, from his lofty course.
In death, his face showed no remorse,
But peace, as if cleansed from evil's source.

Rama, victorious, in his righteous might,
Instructed Matali, to end their flight.
With gratitude and honour, in the celestial light,
He sent him back, to the heavens' height.

For even in death, Rama's goodness shone,
Transforming Ravana, from his tyrant's throne.
In his meditation on Rama, peace was sown,
A tranquil end, in a tone, atone.

RAMA'S VICTORY IN LANKA: ECHOES AND CONSEQUENCES

The Dawn of Righteousness

In the ancient saga, where echoes of battles soar,
Silence descended, as Ravana met his lore.
A timeless war, truth's resounding call,
Divine virtues triumphed, falsehood's reign did befall.

The clash of realms, of right and wrong,
In Rama's hands, destiny's song.
Righteousness stood, valiant and strong,
Unrighteousness was defeated, where it didn't belong.

With Ravana gone, the war did cease,
In its wake, a newfound peace.
Truth's bright sun, on the rise, did increase,
Divine virtues, in their golden fleece.

Rama, the hero, just and fair,
Declared Bivishan, Lanka's heir.
A promise kept, with honour rare,
A new reign of righteousness, in Lanka's lair.

Bivishan, once refuge sought,
In Rama's grace, a kingdom was bought.
A rule of virtue, as he ought,
In the land where battles were fought.

Thus ended the war, of cosmic scale,
Truth and righteousness did prevail.
In the annals of time, an eternal tale,
Where good's mighty ship, set sail.

In this story, where morals align,
Rama's victory, a design divine.
A testament to virtue, a sacred sign,
In the heart of righteousness, forever to shine.

The Joyous Liberation

In the quiet gardens, where Sita stayed,
Came the news that lifted her shade.
Ravana, the captor, by Rama's hand, was slayed,
A dawn of joy, in her heart, brightly laid.

Her heart, aflutter, in happiness soared,
The chains of despair were finally unmoored.
The tyrant's end, by her beloved lord,
A moment of triumph, like a harmonious chord.

Long had she waited, in sorrow's deep well,
Her spirit, enduring, under captivity's spell.
Now, with Ravana's demise, a liberating bell,
Rang through the air, a victorious tell.

Her longing to reunite with her dear Rama,
A love unbroken, amidst life's drama.
At the end of her trials, a healing balm,
A reunion awaited, in serenity's calm.

Beyond measure, her joy did rise,
Like the sun's warm embrace in morning skies.
Her heart raced, with eager eyes,
To behold her lord, her cherished prize.

In her joy, the world seemed to sing,
A melody of freedom, on hope's wing.
Sita, the captive, supposed to be a queen of the king,
In the saga of love, her tale is like a ring.

Thus, the news of victory, a sweet refrain,
Ended her sorrow, her pain, her chain.
In her heart, Rama's love, a constant lane,
Together once more, in happiness' domain.

The Trial and Triumph

In the realm where myths and legends dwell,
Sita's tale, a poignant chapter, does tell.
Her essence, with the fire, did she consign,
Yet faced a trial, to prove her shine.

A test of fire, to show her truth,
Her chastity's proof, in ageless youth.
Into the flames, she bravely stepped,
With faith and honour, her heart adept.

In Agni's (Fire-God's) realm, a tale of mystic creation,
Shadow of Sita was secured, an ethereal revelation.
A Goddess weaves illusion, a spectral guise,
Double of Sita, veiled in divine ties.

At the abduction stage, events unfold,
A real Sita, in Agni's protection, securely holds.
In Agni's embrace, an illusory dance,
One consumed, one emerges, truth's intricate trance.

However, from the fire, Sita emerged, radiant and clear,
Her glory, her divinity was shining, in every sphere.
With purity's light, she stood, so dear,
After a long wait, joining Rama, her husband, near.

Yet, their kingdom lay afar, a distant dream,
Ayodhya, in their hearts, is a constant beam.
To return to their land, their rightful realm,
A celestial chariot, emerged at the helm.

The Pushpak Vimana, the flying chariot, a divine craft,
In its wings, the winds of fate were draft(ed).
To carry them home, through the sky's vast shaft,
A journey of hope, on time's raft.

Thus, from Lanka's isle, they took to the skies,
Soaring over lands, where destiny lies.
Together, united, under celestial eyes,
Bound for Ayodhya, where their future ties.

A tale of trials, love, and return,
In Sita's story, profound lessons burn.
Of strength, purity, a love that yearns,
In the epic's heart, where dharma churns.

To their kingdom, they flew, on wings so grand,
Rama –Sita and Lakshmana, hand in hand.
Through trials and triumphs, they did withstand,
To reign once more, in their beloved land.

The Bond of Brotherhood

In the forest deep, where whispers tell,
Of Bharata's oath, a promise to dwell.
Should Rama tarry, beyond exile's spell,
On pyre's flame, Bharata would farewell.

Rama, in his heart, held Bharata dear,
His brother's love, pure, without fear.
A race against time, drawing near,
To save Bharata, whom he revered.

In urgency, Hanuman took to the skies,
A messenger swift, where his duty lies.
To Bharata, he flew, to convey the ties,
Of Rama's return, under the open skies.

Bharata's love, a flame so bright,
Rama's shoes, on the throne, were a sight.
A symbol of respect, in the kingdom's light,
For his brother, his heart's delight.

Upon hearing the news, joy unbound,
Bharata's heart leaped, a profound sound.
At the border of Ayodhya, he with Satrughna were found,
Where Rama's chariot, would touch the ground.

In anticipation, their hearts did yearn,
For the moment of reunion, to return.
Brothers, separated by fate's stern,
Their bond was unbroken, in love's churn.

The Vimana descended, a sight to behold,
Rama alighted, as the prophecy told.
Four brothers met, in emotions bold,
A story of love, agelessly old.

In their embrace, the world did see,
The power of love was as strong as a tree.
Brotherhood's bond, pure and free,
In four brothers' heart, forever to be.

Their joy, a river, flowing wide,
In the kingdom's heart, they did reside.
Together at last, side by side,
In the flow of love, they took pride.

Thus, in the annals of time, it's penned,
Of a brotherly love, that never did end.
Through trials and time, it did transcend,
A testament to the love that the heavens send.

Odyssey of Exile: Ram's Fourteen-Year Sojourn

From the heart of Ayodhya, where tears were shed,
A prince set forth, destiny's path to tread.
Through the lands and time, his journey spans,
In the age-old tale that through ages fans.

First to Prayag, where rivers meet and sing,
Their waters whispering of a future king.
A confluence of faith, where stories intertwine,
Marking the steps of a lineage divine.

Then to Chitrakut, in nature's embrace,
A haven of serenity, a tranquil place.
Here, amidst the sylvan calm and peace,
Life's tumultuous tides found momentary cease.

Panchavati beckoned, lush and wild,
A forest home, nature's undefiled.
In its depths, a saga took its turn,
Where shadows danced and destiny's fires burn(ed).

Onward to Kishkinda, the realm of ape and stone,
Where alliances were forged, in a world unknown.
Here, in friendship and trust's strong bind,
A force was gathered, one of its kind.

To Rameshwaram, where sands and seas merge,
A bridge of hope, humanity's surge.
Each grain of sand, a testament to will,
Where faith moved mountains, and waters stood still.

Lastly, on the shores of Lanka's land,
Where final battles were fought, and victory was at hand.
A land of legend, where epics close,
And tales of valour to the heavens rose.

Fourteen years, a journey of heart and soul,
Through realms and emotions, towards a destined goal.
In each step, a story, in each land, apart,
Of Rama's eternal journey, a map of the human heart.

The Coronation of Joy: Rama's Return to Ayodhya

In Ayodhya's heart, where hope resides,
A coronation, history's pages bides.
For Rama's return, the city prepares,
A celebration, none other compares.

Fourteen years, of longing spent,
Now culminate in a joyous event.
The streets adorned, with festive garment,
A scene of splendour, in every segment.

The citizens, their hearts alight,
In the presence of Rama, a delightful sight.
Their king returned, in his righteous might,
A dawn of happiness, after a long night.

Courtiers, and family, all gathered near,
The atmosphere was charged with cheer.
Bliss and joy, in the air, so clear,
A moment awaited, year after year.

Rama, with Sita, side by side,
In royal grandeur, their kingdom's pride.
As king and queen, they preside,
In love and duty, forever tied.

Ayodhya rejoiced, in a festive tone,
Their beloved Rama is on the throne.
A city's love, so brightly shown,
In the glow of happiness, newly sown.

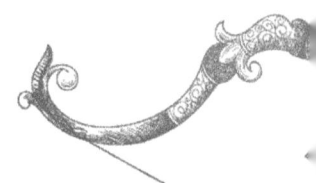

Each corner of the kingdom, in jubilation,
Celebrated Rama's righteous coronation.
A moment of unity, a divine foundation,
For a reign of peace, and a prosperous nation.

Thus, in Ayodhya, joy did reign,
As Rama returned, to his domain.
In every heart, a blissful strain,
The king and queen would rule again.

The Bitter-sweet Farewell

In the wake of jubilation's grand tide,
Came the moment of parting, side by side.
The monkey-force, with hearts open wide,
Faced the farewell, a journey to bide.

Sugriva, Jambuvan, Angada, in tow,
Their faces were shadowed by a sorrowful glow.
Leaving Rama's presence, a blow to their soul,
A departure's toll, taking its toll.

The royal guests, their hearts heavy,
With memories cherished, tender and levy.
None wished to leave the warmth so heady,
Of Rama's grace, steady and ready.

Among them, Hanuman, loyal and true,
His grief profound, as the moment drew.
To leave behind his God, a view askew,
His devotion, a bond forever anew.

Tasked to serve in Kishkindha's land,
Hanuman obeyed, as fate command (ed).
But his heart remained, like a strand,
Tied to Rama, in a bond so grand.

The friends' departure, a scene of mixed emotion(s),
A blend of duty, love, and devotion.
Each step away, like a drop in the ocean,
Of their love for Rama, a deep, vast notion.

Ayodhya's gates, saw their backs turn,
As they left, for their homes, they yearn.
But in their hearts, a flame did burn,
For Rama's love, for his return.

Thus, the farewell, bittersweet in its phase,
Marked by love, in so many ways.
Though they parted, in their gaze,
Lay the promise of meeting, in future days.

UTTAR KANDA: THE ODYSSEY BEYOND

The Serene Realm and Sorrowful Exile

In the calm hues of the Uttara Kanda's day,
Rama, as Vishnu, in tranquil sway,
Reigned in Ayodhya, where stories lay,
Of demon's kin, in Agastya's convey.

Secure and serene, in his kingdom's heart,
Rama listened to tales, an ancient art.
Of Ravana's lineage, a world apart,
In the calm of the 'Kanda', a quiet start.

Yet, in this peace, a storm did brew,
A washer-man's words, harsh and untrue.
His scorn for his wife, in public view,
Cast a shadow on Rama, a painful cue.

The accusation, baseless, yet loud,
Rama, in his dharma, unbowed.
But public opinion, a relentless crowd,
Forced Sita away, under suspicion's shroud.

In Rama's heart, a poignant tear,
Duty's call, love held in fear.
To send Sita, his soul apart,
Kingly duty, a heavy heart.

Laxmana by her side, the forest's lane,
Sita, in shock, felt love's deep pain.
Rama's heart, a silent cry,
As pregnant Sita bid goodbye.

To the forest, Sita returned once more,
Heart heavy, with a painful core.
In Valmiki's ashram, by river Tamsa's shore,
A shelter in sorrow, in folklore.

In nature's cradle, where silence sways,
She birthed twins, Luv and Kush, in quiet bays.
Their innocence, a tranquil brush,
Against the canvas of exile's rush.

This chapter, serene yet steeped in pain,
Echoed Rama's duty, in a poignant strain.
A balance of dharma, hard to sustain,
In the realm of mortals, a challenging domain.

Thus unfolds the tale, in its final part,
A story of love, duty, and a broken heart.
In the Ramayana's pages, an eternal chart,
Of human virtues, and their complex art.

Twin Sons: Sita's Lullaby

In a forest, where whispers of fate entwine,
Dwelt Sita, with love as deep as the divine.
Her heart, a chalice of motherly grace,
Nurturing Lava and Kusha, in life's embrace.

Tender, kind, reflections of her soul's light,
Raised in shadows, yet shining ever bright.
Sita's sons, in wisdom and kindness dressed,
Mirrors of a mother, by life's trials pressed.

Eyes of a mother, worn by time's decree,
Yet in her sons, life's beauty she could see.
Loving a husband, revered as divine,
Enduring injustice, yet refusing to pine.

In her heart, a tale of love and loss,
A life of tribulations, a heavy cross.
Yet, in Lava and Kusha, hope resonates,
Sita's love, through time, it permeates.

In this ballad of a mother's silent plea,
Lies a story of love, loss, and destiny.
A tale of resilience, strength, and fight,
Sita's journey, a beacon in the night.

Luv and Kush: Blossoming Under Guru's Guidance

In the woods, where ancient whispers weave,
Valmiki took to teach, to guide, to conceive.
Luv and Kush, in innocence, did receive,
Lessons of archery, in which to believe.

At the tender age of five, so young,
Their training began, songs unsung.
In the art of the bow, their prowess sprung,
With arrows swift, from their fingers flung.

Speed of sound, their arrows flew,
A sight to behold, in morning's dew.
Raised unaware of their lineage true,
In the art of war, they keenly grew.

Valmiki, wise, in celestial lore,
Taught them warfare, God's core.
Divine tactics, strategies, and more,
Masters of archery, in their heart's store.

In their veins, the blood of kings,
Yet in their hearts, simple things.
Unaware of their royal strings,
In the forest, their talent sings.

No warrior on earth, could them defeat,
In archery's art, they were elite.
With every target, they would meet,
Their skill in battle, none could beat.

Thus, under Valmiki's watchful eye,
Luv and Kush, destined to fly high.
In the art of war, they did not shy,
Born to be heroes, under the sky.

In this tale of tutelage and might,
Two princes grew, hidden from sight.
In the sage's care, they found their light,
Ready for a future, brilliantly bright.

The Challenge of Destiny: The Ashwamedha and the Princes

In Ayodhya's realm, where dharma reigns,
Rama's rule, in its righteous chains,
Undertook the Ashwamedha, a ritual grand,
To expand his kingdom, over the land.

A horse, a symbol of imperial might,
Sent forth, in regal flight,
To nearby kingdoms, a sight,
A choice of annexation or a fight.

With a mighty army, the horse roamed free,
A challenge of power, a royal decree.
To accept subjugation, or to disagree,
A test of sovereignty's key.

Into the forest, where secrets sleep,
The horse wandered, in the green so deep.
Where Luv and Kush, under Valmiki's keep,
Lived in ignorance, in innocence steep.

The twin princes, unaware of the rite,
Saw the horse, in their playful sight.
Tied it up, in their youthful might,
Oblivious to its imperial light.

Unknowing the symbol, of Rama's quest,
In their simple act, a new test.
A collision of fates, in their nest,
In the saga of time, a chapter's crest.

Thus began a tale, unforeseen,
Of princes and a king, in a scene.
The Ashwamedha, a ritual keen,
In the hands of destiny, a serene.

In this twist of fate, where paths collide,
Luv and Kush, in their youthful stride,
Faced a challenge, wide and tide,
In the grand tale of Rama, their role implied.

The Encounter of Rama and His Sons

In the verdant woods, where destiny's hand weaves,
Came Hanuman, on a quest through the leaves.
To retrieve the horse, a mission he perceives,
But fate, in its craft, a different story conceives.

Luv and Kush, princes unaware,
Caught Hanuman in their innocent snare.
Tied him up, with a youthful flair,
While he meditated, Rama's name in his prayer.

Rama, perturbed, his brothers sent,
To unravel the mystery, on his intent.
Upon the scene, their gaze they bent,
Hanuman captive, an unexpected event.

They saw the boys, guardians of the steed,
Mistook their act, for a thievish deed.
A battle ensued, in a dramatic lead,
But Luv and Kush, in skill, did exceed.

The princes fought, with courage and might,
Defeated their uncles, in the fading light.
Rama, informed, sensed the plight,
A hermitage's children, winning the fight.

Rama, the king, to the forest came,
To face the challengers, to preserve his fame.
Yet unknown to him, the tie, the same,
His sons stood before him, in life's game.

The Valiant Young Hearts

In the realm where legends softly tread,
Rama stood, in awe and wonder spread.
Before him, two boys, brave and small,
Defiant in spirit, standing tall.

A challenge thrown, a childish fray,
To return the horse, in a playful way.
Yet, in their eyes, a fire did burn,
A refusal bold, at every turn.

As Rama's bow, with might, was drawn,
An arrow poised, from dawn to dawn.
To discipline, with a warrior's art,
But fate had planned a different part.

Sage Valmiki, wisdom's guiding light,
Stepped forth in the escalating fight.
"Avoid divine wrath on these young souls," he said,
"They are but children, by innocence led."

He spoke to the brothers, with gentle might,
To return the horse, and set all right.
In reverence, they obeyed their sage,
Their actions were wise, beyond their age.

With the horse returned, peace did reign,
Rama's journey towards the forest was not in vain.
With brothers at the side, in unity's embrace,
Back to Ayodhya, with dignified grace.

Thus ended the clash, of young and old,
A tale of bravery, courageously told.
In the heart of history, forever will reside,
The day youthful valour, with wisdom, did collide.

The Ballad of Destiny: Luv and Kush's Revelation

In the quiet of a forest, veiled in time's embrace,
Lava and Kusha stood, with innocence on their face.
To their mother, they recounted the tale,
Of courage and valour, that would never pale.

Sita, heart-struck by the story's fold,
Revealed to them a truth untold.
Their lineage, a secret, now brought to light,
In their hearts, a new purpose took flight.

Indignant for justice, they yearned to depart,
To seek their father, with an aching heart.
But wise Valmiki, with a calming sway,
Urged them to sing the Ramayana's lay.

In Ayodhya's streets, their voices rang clear,
Verses of sorrow, for all to hear.
The citizens wept, moved by the song,
Feeling Sita's pain, deep and strong.

Rama, upon hearing this soulful plea,
Summoned the boys to his court, to see.
Captivated by the epic's profound grace,
He marvelled at its beauty, in that sacred place.

"How do these young souls know my life's story?"
He wondered, amidst his own heart's quarry.
His spirit cried for Sita, his life, his lost love,
As the tale unfolded, just like a divine glove.

Then, the revelation, like a thunderous wave,
"We're your offspring," their courage gave.
Lava and Kusha, of royal blood,
In their veins, the legacy of a flood.

Thus, the echo of destiny found its way,
In the hearts of a family, long astray.
A ballad of unity, from discord's night,
Brought together by truth's revealing light.

The Reunion of Hearts

A father's heart, in sudden wake,
Longed for Sita, for their love's sake.
To Valmiki's ashram, his journey to make,
For his wife, his soul, in ache.

Through forest paths, in quiet dread,
Rama walked, where fate had led.
To the sage's abode, his heart was sped,
To meet Sita, where his love was bred.

In the sanctuary, where serenity lies,
Rama beheld Sita, with tearful eyes.
A reunion of hearts, under the vast skies,
A moment of truth, where love never dies.

There, in the quiet of the sage's realm,
Rama found Sita, like a guiding helm.
In the presence of his love, overwhelmed,
In the ashram's peace, his fears to whelm.

Thus, in the journey to the sage's door,
Rama found what he was searching for.
A family tended to reunite, in lore,
In the heart of the ashram, love's evermore.

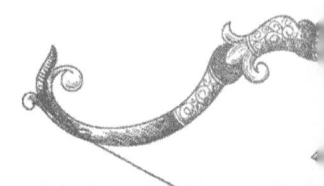

The Test of Truth: Sita's Second Ordeal

In Ayodhya's realm, where whispers stir,
Came the question of purity, a societal blur.
Rama, in his heart, knew Sita pure,
Yet the people's doubt, he had to endure.

"O sage of virtue, let it be so,"
Rama declared, in a voice low.
"Sita's innocence, I fully know,
But to quell the whispers, to and fro."

Sita, once tested by fire's embrace,
Now faced another trial, in public space.
Rama, torn, in a painful case,
Sought to restore her honour, her grace.

The Gods assembled, a celestial crowd,
Brahma leading, heads bowed.
All the Gods and Deities were not loud,
To witness of Sita's defence, proud.

Rama affirmed, in the assembly's sight,
"Valmiki's words hold the light.
I wish to reconcile, make right,
With Vaidehi (Sita), my heart's plight."

The assembly, emotional, in rapt attention,
Awaited Sita's moment, a divine intervention.
Vayu, the Wind-God, in his ascension,
Brought a breeze of purity, a heavenly mention.

A fragrance pure, the air did fill,
A sign of divine, a sacred thrill.
As in the Golden Age, a wonder still,
To the gathered throng, a joyous spill.

Sita, in her grace, stood serene,
Amidst the Gods, a sight unseen.
Her truth and purity, evergreen,
In the test of fire, once again keen.

Thus, in the eyes of Gods and men,
Sita proved her honour, once again.
Her honour unblemished, she did sustain,
In the test of truth, her purity's reign.

The Earth's Embrace: Sita's Divine Ascent

In the assembly's midst, Sita stood so brave,
Clad in yellow, her demeanor grave.
With palms joined, her plea she gave,
"To Mother earth's heart, if true I've stayed."

As her words echoed, a wonder unfurled,
From the earth, a throne, like a pearl.
Nagas bore it, in a powerful swirl,
Adorned with gems, a celestial whirl.

Dharani, Earth Goddess, in grace appeared,
Welcomed Sita, as the assembly cheered.
On that throne, Sita, revered,
In blossoms' shower, her path cleared.

Seated high, in the celestial seat,
Sita's journey is complete and sweet.
A divine ascent, a feat so neat,
In her mother's arms, her destiny meet.

Lament of Innocence: Grief-stricken Lava- Kusha

In the realm of heartache, where tears silently fall,
Lava and Kusha wept, in grief's inconsolable call.
Their world, their mother, and the endless love she gave,
In her embrace, every mischief she forgave.

She, the heartbeat of her two tender sons,
Her love, a river that endlessly runs.
Valmiki, their guardian, wise and kind,
Yet their hearts for their mother pined.

Their tears, like rivers, carved paths of pain,
Seeking her presence, in loss's unyielding chain.
From the earth, they yearned for her return,
A longing deep, where silent sorrows burn.

But fate, a cruel script, unyielding and stark,
Left them searching in the endless dark.
Rama, their father, in an embrace tight,
Tried to soothe their souls, in sorrow's night.

Yet, how could their young hearts understand,
The void left by her absent hand?
How to live, when from love they're torn?
In their fate, such cruel thorns were born.

Unknown to them, was their father's face,
And now their mother, lost in time's embrace.
A twist of destiny, so harsh and grim,
Leaving their world, on a sorrowful brim.

In this tale of loss, where innocence grieves,
Lies the story of two leaves, shaken from life's trees.
Lava and Kusha, in their youthful plight,
A portrait of love, lost in fate's blight.

Their cries, a testament to love's deep cost,
In the maelstrom of fate, innocently tossed.
A story of love, separation, and fate's cruel game,
In the saga of life, where nothing remains the same.

RAMA'S VOYAGE INTO THE INFINITE

The Golden Epoch: Rama's Reign of Harmony

In the reign of Rama, a tale of peace,
He appointed kin, for harmony's lease.
Throughout India, from west to east,
His rule, a perfect administration's feast.

Brothers and successors, in regions afar,
Upheld his ideals, like a guiding star.
In his realm, no crime to mar,
Only harmony, near and far.

A truthful aura, in the air did dwell,
In every corner, a peaceful spell.
Rama Rajya, a land of truth, as stories tell,
A rare moment, where righteousness fell.

Known for dharma, prosperity's hand,
Peace pervaded, over the land.
In history's epochs, a period grand,
Rama's rule was like a golden band.

In this era, the world did see,
A reign of justice, pure and free.
A legacy of peace, in its highest degree,
Rama's epoch, an eternal decree.

The Twilight of Destiny: Rama and Lakshmana's Sacrifice

In Ayodhya's court, where questions rise,
Why Rama left for Vaikuntha's skies.
Ancient texts, in their wise disguise,
Shed light on this tale, where mystery lies.

One day, a sage, old and bent,
Sought Rama's ear, with intent.
In private chambers, their time was spent,
Lakshmana guarded, his duty lent.

Rama's command, firm and vast,
"None shall pass," a decree cast.
Lakshmana, loyal, stood at the gate,
His dedication, a brother's fate.

The visitor, none other than 'Time',
Cloaked in wisdom, truth sublime;
Announcing Rama's destined end,
A celestial journey, to ascend.

Then Durvasa, in sudden stride,
Demanded entry, couldn't be denied.
Lakshmana, in turmoil, deep inside,
A brother's love, his only guide.

To save Rama, from Durvasa's curse,
Lakshmana chose his fate to traverse.
Entered the room, the universe terse,
A sacrifice made, in silent verse.

Rama, distraught, a promise to keep,
Kala Deva's (Time-God) word, a pit so deep.
Lakshmana's exile, a decision steep,
A verdict of pain, to make hearts weep.

Thus, the brothers, noble and true,
Faced their destiny, in a twilight's hue.
Rama to Vaikuntha, Lakshmana anew,
In sacrifice and love, their legend grew.

Embark on the Celestial Voyage

In the shadow of destiny's grand design,
Lakshmana knew, that without Rama, no sunshine.
Part of one soul, in celestial line,
Without his brother, he could not confine.

A bond so deep, in cosmic twine,
Lakshmana chose Jal Samadhi, a sign.
To join Rama, in the divine shrine,
His earthly role, he did resign.

The Time-God spoke, in tones so fine,
"Sita awaits in Vaikuntha, align.
You, next in line, for duties divine,
In Rama's service, your stars entwine."

Jal Samadhi, the water's embrace,
Lakshmana entered, with tranquil grace.
Leaving the world, a mortal race,
For Vaikuntha, his eternal place.

Rama, left alone, in his kingdom's heart,
Fulfilled his roles, in every part.
A brother, father, a divine chart,
His time on earth, now to depart.

Having vanquished Ravana, the demon of night,
Established Rama-Rajya, a realm of right.
His duties done, in dharma's light,
It was time to leave, and end his earthly fight.

He knew his path, to Vaikuntha's door,
His earthly journey, needed no more.
In leaving, he closed a sacred lore,
His legacy, a legend, forevermore.

The Divine Departure: Lord Rama's Journey to Eternity

In Ayodhya's heart, where faith resides,
Lord Rama announced, as destiny guides.
His kingdom to kin, he did confide,
Preparing to leave, with time's tide.

His subjects gathered, in love and plea,
"Take us with you," their heartfelt decree.
Rama, compassionate, set their souls free,
Granted moksha, the final key.

Towards the Sarayu, they walked in grace,
Each step is a march towards the sacred space.
Into the river's embrace, they did face,
Disappeared they all, without a trace.

So ended the Treta Yuga's span,
Etched in memories, since time began.
Rama and his people, in a divine plan,
Returned to the heavens, as it ran.

In unique ways, their paths were set,
Predestined, predetermined, without regret.
In the annals of history, never to forget,
Lord Rama's journey, a celestial bet.

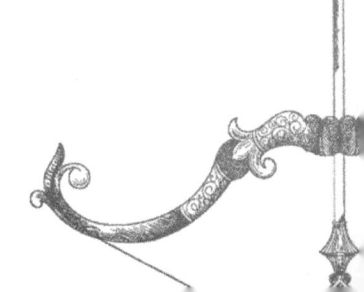

UNVEILING RAMA AND SITA'S SACRED LOVE

Celestial Union: The Divine Love of Rama and Sita

In the cosmic vastness where stars whisper lore,
Dwells a tale of divinity, etched in ancient yore.
A celestial union, a sacred rite,
Where Rama and Sita, in divine light, ignite.

Rama, the Vishnu incarnate, bearer of truth,
His essence of righteousness, eternal and couth.
In the forest of existence, his valour shines bright,
Guiding the lost, with his unwavering light.

And Sita, the embodiment of Lakshmi's grace,
Her aura of compassion, time cannot efface.
In the garden of virtues, her love blooms like a flower,
Showering blessings, in every sunlit hour.

In a cosmic ballet, together they sway,
On the universe's stage, where stars play.
Their union transcends the mortal's sight,
A fusion of souls, in celestial light.

Protectors of dharma, the cosmic law,
Their love, a testament, without flaw.
In their embrace, the universe finds its rhyme,
Their sacred love, divine-bond, transcends time.

In every heartbeat of the cosmos, their story is sung,
Of Rama and Sita, forever young.
A reminder to all, of the divine play,
Where love and duty, in harmony lay.

For in their union, the heavens rejoice,
The universe echoes with their unified voice.
Teaching us the essence of cosmic function,
In their eternal, divine conjunction.

The Eternal Vows

In the hallowed halls of time, where legends dwell,
A tale of love and devotion, the bards do tell.
Rama and Sita, in sacred union bound,
Their hearts in harmony, a love profound.

With vows of eternal devotion, under heaven's gaze,
They pledged to wander life's intricate maze.
Only to each other, their souls did yearn,
A flame of love, forever to burn.

Yet fate's cruel hand, in unforeseen ways,
Cast Rama to forests, in solitude's haze.
In exile, he wandered, a prince without throne,
But in his heart, Sita's love shone.

Through verdant woods and silent glades,
Their love, a beacon that never fades.
For Rama, Sita's well-being was his creed,
Her happiness, his only need.

In the whispers of leaves, in the sigh of the breeze,
Their love was as deep as the endless seas.
For in every step, every breath of air,
Rama's devotion was beyond compare.

This tale, a lesson, in love's pure art,
To place our beloved, above our own heart.
For in the dance of life, with its twists and turns,
True love is the flame that forever burns.

In fleeting joy, Rama and Sita did entwine,
Briefly together, then parting, love divine.
Yet, in their hearts, a flame that forever sighed,
For eternal love, in separation, never died.

In the celestial script, Sita took her early flight,
To heavenly realms, where eternal stars alight.
Ram, in sorrow, bore the pain each day,
Till his journey's end, in twilight's soft array.

Let the "Ramayana's" model couple be our guide,
In love's journey, let their spirit reside.
For to endure, to stand the test of time,
Love must be selfless, pure, and sublime.

So let us learn from Rama and his bride,
To cherish love, with hearts open wide.
For in the end, when all is done and said,
It's love that triumphs, in every story read.

The Crow and the Compassionate: A Tale of Love and Mercy

Once, upon Chitrakuta's serene height,
Rama and Sita, in love's light.
A crow, in hunger's desperate plight,
Attacked Sita, a distressing sight.

Her pain echoed, through the hill's air,
Rama, her protector, couldn't bear.
With kusha- grass, an arrow to prepare,
A bramhastra (strong weapon), in righteous flare.

The crow, in fear, took to the sky,
With divine arrow, close by.
Around the world, its desperate cry,
From Rama's wrath, it could not fly.

In the end, to Rama, it did yield,
Seeking mercy, on the battlefield.
But a brahmastra, once in the field,
Cannot retract, its fate sealed.

Yet Rama, in his compassion's might,
Modified the curse, in his sight.
To spare the crow, from its plight,
One eye struck, in the arrow's flight.

In this tale, love and mercy blend,
Rama and Sita, love without end.
An epic story, messages send,
Of compassion's power, to amend.

Love Unbound

In the realm where heartbeats echo with nature's song,
There dwelled Sita, where love and earth belong.
Her spirit, a melody in sync with wild's choir,
A bond with nature, kindled by love's fire.

In her heart, a love for Rama, pure and deep,
A devotion so profound, it could make the heavens weep.
Her soul's frequency, with nature's rhythm aligned,
In every leaf's rustle, Rama's image was enshrined.

By Ganga's sacred waters, under the sky so wide,
Sita's prayers flowed, with the ebbing tide.
To protect her beloved from the forest's harsh decree,
She beckoned nature's guardians, on bended knee.

Yet, when darkness came, in Ravana's vile hand,
She called to the earth, the sky, the sea, and the land.
To rivers that meander, to birds that soar,
An appeal to save her from evil to the core.

Trees wept in distress, their sorrow a silent plea,
Unable to shield her from her horrific destiny.
Animals mourned, their spirits in despair,
At the sight of her plight, too much to bear.

The earth itself, in a trance of grief,
Felt the weight of sorrow, stark and brief.
In her plea, the old vulture Jatayu awoke,
Against Ravana, in valour, he spoke.

In his final breath, a hero's fight he gave,
Falling in honour, noble and brave.
And as Sita scattered her jewels in haste,
A path for Rama, in the wilderness traced.

Monkeys gathered the gems, a clue to her fate,
Joining Rama's quest, before it was too late.
In every whisper of wind, every wave's crest,
Lay Sita's love for Rama, her eternal quest.

So let the tale be told, of love's enduring might,
Of Sita, nature's guardian, in darkness and light.
A love that called to the earth and the skies,
In harmony's embrace, where true love lies.

Echoes of Separation: Rama's Lament for Sita

In the hush of ancient woods, where whispers speak,
Lies a tale of love, in sorrow's mystique.
Rama, heart laden with a heavy sigh,
Found Sita's anklet, under the sky.

A solitary gem, lost and apart,
Mirroring the ache in Rama's heart.
Like a silent sentinel, it lay,
Mourning the absence, where once she'd stray.

"It is here," he murmured, "her step's grace,
This hallowed ground, our love's embrace."
The anklet, a symbol of their severed bond,
In its silence, their unspoken fond.

As if in grief, it refused to sing,
Longing for the touch of Sita's being.
Each gem and jingle, a story of loss,
A tale of love, and its cruel cost.

Rama's eyes, with tears unshed,
Spoke of the pain of separation, unsaid.
In Kalidasa's verses, the pain unfolds,
A story of love, in time's eternal holds.

For in the anklet's quiet, a lament was found,
A symbol of love, in sorrow bound.
Rama and Sita, in destiny's weave,
A story of separation that poets conceive.

Tears of Malyavata Peaks: Rama's Silent Witness

In the shadow of Malyavata's ancient peaks,
Where nature listens and silence speaks,
Rama's heart, heavy with unshed tears,
Whispered of love, through the passing years.

To Sita, he conveyed, in words unspoken,
His heart's sorrow, a bond unbroken.
The mountain stood, a silent confessor,
Bearing witness to his silent pressure.

As if the rocks themselves could feel,
The depth of Rama's love, was so real.
They wept with him, in a sympathy's embrace,
Releasing rain, like tears on Earth's face.

Each drop, a testament to his pain,
Echoing his longing, again and again.
Malyavata, in its ancient, stoic grace,
Mirrored Rama's heart in its own base.

This tale, a poignant dance of nature and heart,
Symbolizing Rama's sorrow, an artistic part.
The mountain's rain, like a symphony of grief,
Offering in its way, a silent relief.

In the love of Rama and Sita, pure and true,
Lay a life of joy, before darkness grew.
Their shared happiness, a memory dear,
In the rain of Malyavata, crystal clear.

A story of love, etched in nature's guise,
Where every raindrop, a symbol of ties.
In the tears of a mountain, and a lover's sigh,
Lies a tale of love, that never dies.

The Paragon of Virtues: Ram's Multifaceted Love

In the epic's breadth, where virtues shine,
Stands Ram, a hero, in every line.
As son, brother, king, his roles align,
But as husband, his love's divine design.

Morally firm, yet tenderly mild,
With Sita, his heart was never beguiled.
The golden deer, a request compiled,
He pursued, by love's plea, gently styled.

Indulgent partner, caring and wise,
In Sita's wish, no deceit or guise.
Though aware of the demon's lies,
For her smile, to the challenge, he flies.

Yet, in this act, love's sad twist,
Sita's abduction, in fate's cruel mist.
Ram's proof of love, in history's list,
A tale of devotion, time can't resist.

In Ram, a portrait of love's many hues,
A saga of choices, a path to muse.
Heroic yet tender, his love imbues,
A journey through life's complex views.

In Forests Deep: Sita's Unwavering Journey

In the echoes of an ancient decree, destiny was spun,
For Rama, the prince, forest exile begun.
Fourteen years, a journey through time and space,
In the wilderness, a test of faith and grace.

But Sita, his queen, in her heart a resolute fire,
Refused the comforts of a regal spire.
For her place, she knew, was by his side,
In the forest deep, where shadows reside.

With love as her armour, devotion as her shield,
She stepped into the woods, her fate sealed.
To wander with Rama, through thicket and thorn,
In untamed wilds, where legends are born.

Rama, in reluctance, sought to dissuade,
His heart in turmoil, his decision swayed.
But Sita, with steadfast spirit and unyielding will,
Stood firm with Ram, her duty to fulfill.

In the quiet of the woods, under the canopy's embrace,
They found a world of untold grace.
Every leaf whispered tales of yore,
Each dawn brought wonders, unexplored.

Together they trod, through trials untold,
Their bond of love was a sight to behold.
In the dance of the fireflies, the rustle of leaves,
Their love was a testament that heart believes.

In the solitude of the forest, time stood still,
Their journey, a testament of love and will.
For Sita chose not the path of ease,
But the trail where love's true essence frees.

So let this tale, in the annals of time, be cast,
Of love that endures, of vows that last.
For in the heart of the forest, so deep and so wide,
Lies the story of Sita, her unwavering stride.

The Hour of Separation: The Moment of Despair

In the wake of loss, where silence screams,
Rama returned, to a world sans dreams.
Sita gone, a heart that teems,
With grief so deep, it unredeems.

In the poets' words, echoed true,
Love's depth, in absence, in view.
Rama's soul, torn in two,
Shattered, bereft, in sorrow's hue.

In his grief, he roamed, a ghost,
Asking nature, his heart's lost host.
His will to live, a fading post,
In the shadow of love's daunting cost.

Who among the heartbroken, can't relate,
To Rama's despair, a cruel fate.
In his agony, a desolate state,
A love lost, a heavy slate.

Lakshman, with wisdom, intervened,
Awakening Rama, from grief so keen.
A man with a mission, newly gleaned,
In love's trial, his purpose weaned.

A pivotal moment, in love's long story,
From the depths of despair to a quest for glory.
Rama and Sita's path, intricate and hoary,
A turning point, in the epic's inventory.

The Dual Role of Rama: Love and Duty

In the saga of Rama, where virtues align,
His defense of Sita, both tender and fine.
Against crow or demon, his actions shine,
A lover and husband, in love's design.

Yet, as a king, his choices weigh,
Agnipareeksha, the fore-test, Sita's dismay.
His heart torn, in a painful fray,
Love and duty, in a tangled array.

Banished Sita, for his subjects' sake,
His heartbreak, a silent quake.
Rama's duty to his land, he could not forsake,
For the kingdom's harmony, his love was at stake.

With no other by his side,
Sita's golden image, his silent bride.
In rituals, his love, he can't hide,
Mocked for loyalty, in the stride he bide(s).

To be Rama, a task so grim,
In love and duty, a constant hymn.
A balance of heart and rule, on a brim,
A king and lover, in history's trim.

Resilient Grace: Sita's Unyielding Love

In the shadowed realm of Lanka, under Ravana's leer,
Stood Sita, a figure of grace, devoid of fear.
Her love for Rama, a beacon so bright,
Shone against the darkness, a flame of light.

Ravana, in his delusion, professed a love unrefined,
But Sita, the swan, his advances declined.
She mocked him, a duck by the shore,
Her grace unswayed, her spirit soared.

In Lanka's land, her valour unfurled,
A fearless woman in a daunting world.
Against the stereotype of submission and frailty,
She stood, a bastion of strength and reality.

Her defiance, a fire, Ravana enraged,
A battle of wills, across the ages waged.
Around eleven and half months he gave, a time to bend,
But her resolve stood firm, till the very end.

In the grove of Ashoka, amidst torment and sneer,
Sita's calm was unbroken, her heart was clear.
Tortured by demons, scorned by the vile,
Yet her soul remained untouched, her spirit agile.

Her harmony with nature, a shield so divine,
Gave her the fortitude, through the dark to shine.
Against Ravana's terror, and his demons' might,
She stood unshaken, a beacon of light.

To Ravana, she spoke, with clarity and might,
Her words cutting through the dark of night.
Inseparable from Rama, like sunlight from the sun,
Her devotion unwavering, till all was done.

In her unity with nature, her strength was found,
A bond so deep, so intensely profound.
Nature's embrace, her fortress so grand,
Against Lanka's devils, she took her stand.

Her belief unshaken, that Rama would come,
To vanquish the evil, to beat the unholy drum.
In her heart, there was a song of hope and faith,
A melody of love, transcending wraith.

In the archives of time, let it be known,
Of Sita's love for Rama, eternally sown.
In nature's arms, her spirit did thrive,
A testament of love, forever alive.

The Unwavering Love of Rama

In an age where kings sought many a bride,
Rama's heart for Sita, could not subside.
Though pain of separation did inside abide,
Thoughts of another union, he did deride.

His love for Sita, pure and unswayed,
Unlike his father, a singular path he laid.
In his silent fortress of sorrow, he stayed,
For her, his heart's melody played.

Though kingdoms around multiple marriages saw,
Rama's devotion to Sita held all in awe.
In her absence, he followed a higher law,
His love was always a never-ending draw.

A testament to fidelity, in times of yore,
Rama's love was permanent, an eternal lore.
In the face of loss, his heart did soar,
Sita, his queen, forevermore.

The Resilience of Sita: A Love Unyielding

In the dance of fate, where Sita stands,
Her silence, a choice, in love's demands.
Not mere obedience in her hands,
But a fiery spirit, in life's sands.

Her acquiescence was not submission's guise,
But a testament of love, that was pure and wise.
In her quiet suffering, her spirit flies,
For love's cause, her heart complies.

Sita, aware of Rama's deep affection,
Values their bond, in its reflection.
Rejects Ravana's threats, his deception,
In Ayodhya's memory, her direction.

Through trials, her marital vow she keeps,
In love's garden, where sorrow seeps.
Her commitment, a river, runs deep,
In the pact of marriage, her promises leap.

Sita, a symbol of strength and love's enduring might,
Through tempests fierce, she always stands upright.
Her resilience, like a blooming flower,
In the annals of time, forever a tower.

THE CONTEMPORARY RELEVANCE OF THE RAMAYANA

The Eternal Saga: Rama's Legacy

In time's ancient scrolls, where legends reside,
Echoes the saga of Rama, in the Ramayana's pride.
A handbook of virtues, in its display,
His life, a sermon, in the cosmic play.

Emperor he reigned, in the Indian land,
For centuries, with a just hand.
From Ayodhya's throne, his command,
After exile's trial, where his faith did stand.

His story, a beacon, through ages told,
Of values, courage, and virtues bold.
In every chapter, his tale unfolds,
Rama's legacy, in hearts, it holds.

Through time's passage, his reign endures,
In the saga of life, his spirit assures.
In the Ramayana's verses, his memory lures,
A timeless emperor, his essence pure.

Echoes of Dharma: The Timeless Wisdom

In life's grand chessboard, where destinies intertwine,
Stands the saga of Rama, a narrative divine.
A tale not just of valour, but of duty's call,
Where Dharma's echoes, in every heart, doth fall.

For in Rama's journey, we find the sacred triad,
Duties of self, family, society, in harmony clad.
Each step, a lesson, in life's intricate dance,
Urging us to embrace duty, in every circumstance.

Rama, an ocean of compassion, love's purest form,
Through his saga, the coldest hearts to warm.
Only through love can his divinity be traced,
In love's gentle waters, life's true meaning embraced.

For love is the undercurrent, life's silent hymn,
In its depths, humanity's light never gets dim.
Man's divinity unveiled, in love's nurturing tide,
Where virtues like pearls, in depths reside.

In modernity's maze, where chaos reigns supreme,
Ramayana's justice (Dharma) is a guiding beam.
In a world where kinship threads may fray,
Rama's ideals gleam as a rare, healing ray.

Where offspring drifts from paternal/maternal grace,
And parents' hearts forget the future's face.
Where gurus seek respect, but may find naught,
And students' reverence may be easily bought.

In this tumult, Ramayana's wisdom, a lighthouse stands,
Illuminating the duties, in life's shifting sands.
It speaks of bonds, of brother, father, mother, son,
Of guru and disciple, until life's course is run.

In realms of business, education, in all those spheres,
Where corruption's shadow, ominously leers.
Ramayana's principles, a moral compass, true,
Guiding society to a path, righteous and due.

It teaches human values, deep and profound,
In its verses, life's true essence is found.
A call to uphold what is just and right,
In the darkest hours, be a beacon of light.

So let us turn the pages of this epic grand,
And in the light of Rama's wisdom, take a stand.
For in Ramayana's teachings, we find our way,
To a brighter, nobler, more virtuous day.

The Lessons of Unity

Upon this Earth, our shared abode,
Under the same sky, our stories unfold.
Breathing one air, drinking one stream,
Yet, in diversity, we lose the unity dream.

The Ramayana, an epic of ancient times,
Speaks of unity, in its verses and rhymes.
In diversity's myriad shades, it finds a single thread,
A lesson of oneness, in numerous tales spread.

In the kaleidoscope of human hues,
Unity fades in life's daily muse.
Lost in a sea of difference and strife,
Forgetting the unity that underpins life.

In Bharat's culture, a wisdom so old,
In words of kindness, truth is told.
Speak truth, yet gentle, never harsh,
In such words, the universe's melody is arched.

Sathyam bruyath(speak the truth), the moral's core,
Priyam bruyath (speak pleasantly),the social values soar.
'Na bruyath sathyam apriyam' - the spiritual guide,
In these ancient words, the three virtues reside.

The Ramayana, in simplicity, imparts,
These values deep, in all our hearts.
But man, adrift, forgets its core,
Wandering like Ravana, on life's shore.

Ravana, with knowledge vast, but heart astray,
Succumbed to desires, lost his way.
His end, a testament to unchecked yearn,
A kingdom lost, a life burnt.

"O people," he cried, in his final breath,
"Chase not desires, for they lead to death.
Be like Rama, in truth and right,
In his path, find the divine light."

So let us learn, from Rama's grace,
To see unity in every face.
To uphold truth, in love and light,
In our shared humanity, find our might.

Thus, in the Ramayana's timeless tale,
Lies a path where truth and love prevail.
A call to unity, in diversity's dance,
In this ancient wisdom, let us find our chance.

Berries of Devotion: Shabari's Timeless Offering

In the whispering woods, where shadows play,
And the sun weaves gold through the leafy fray,
There lived a soul, pure as the driven snow,
Shabari, whose heart with love did glow.

For years she waited, silent and still,
Her spirit steadfast, unbreakable will,
For Rama, her lord, in whom faith she found,
In the quiet grove, where life abound.

Berries she gathered, with tender care,
Each one a gem, precious and rare,
Her offering simple, from the forest floor,
Awaiting the one whom she did adore.

Then came the day, under the sun's gentle beam,
When Rama arrived, like a dream within a dream,
Shabari, with joy, her offering did present,
Berries, mere berries, yet with love they were bent.

Rama, with a smile, graced her humble abode,
Accepting her gift, on this sacred road,
Eating the berries, with reverence and grace,
In the hermit's heart, he found his place.

In this simple act, a truth did unfurl,
A lesson profound, more precious than pearl,
Devotion's pure light, in the simplest of things,
The love one offers, on heartfelt wings.

In Shabari's offering, a story untold,
Of unwavering faith, more valued than gold,
A beacon for us, in life's complex thread,
It's the love we share, in every step we tread.

In Shabari's tender submission, a tale unfolds,
Where caste distinctions, the heart beholds.
A noble soul, in love and grace,
Accepts devotion, in any time or space.

Beyond the bounds of region and creed,
Love's essence fulfils every need.
 Be it riches or in poverty's strife,
Only devotion and purity define a noble life.

Greatness of Mother Sumitra

In the fleeting dance of worldly affairs,
Where change is constant, and few things bear.
Remember, only the Divine stands forever true,
Immutable, pure, eternal, the immortal hue.

So lend your hours to the hymns of the divine,
In the glory of God, let your days entwine.
For in sincere prayer, a revelation awaits,
The discovery of divinity, that in you resonates.

As Lakshmana prepared, for the forest to depart,
Sumitra counselled with wisdom, from the heart.
"Think not of the woods, but of Rama's grace,
Wherever they dwell, that is your sacred place.

Ayodhya without them, a forest forlorn,
In their presence, a haven reborn.
See in Sita and Rama, your parents divine,
Serve them with love, let your devotion shine."

In this world, none greater than Sumitra found,
A mother whose wisdom was profoundly sound.
She blessed her son, to serve the Lord with zeal,
In devotion and faith, her guidance surreal.

Sumitra, a name that echoes 'good friend',
A beacon of virtue, on whom we depend.
Such noble souls, in this age, we seek,
Mothers like her, strong, wise, and meek.

And sons like Lakshmana, in devotion so pure,
Whose love for the Divine does eternally endure.
In their footsteps, let us tread the path,
Of love, sincerity, and a faith that lasts.

Hence, in their story, a timeless lesson rings,
Of devotion to Supreme, and the peace it brings.
In a world of transience, their legacy stays,
A testament to devotion, in all their ways.

In Love's Divine Path

Mother Kaikeyi's wish, a throne for her son,
Yet Bharata, in humility, wanted none.
At Chitrakoota's base, in reverence deep,
He implored Rama, the crown to keep.

But Rama, firm in duty's sacred call,
Upheld his father's word, above all.
"Obey thy parents," he gently said,
A path of righteousness, he always led.

In this, Rama's truthfulness brightly shone,
A beacon of integrity, universally known.
Adhering to truthful speech, his title of grace,
A legacy of truth, for all human race.

Yet in modern times, the Ramayana read,
Its essence lost, its lessons unheeded.
Knowledge amassed, yet wisdom scarce,
In the practice of Dharma, a gap so harsh.

For what use are words, if not lived in deed?
Like unsavoured sweets, they fulfil no need.
Information alone, no transformation brings,
In action alone, wisdom truly sings.

In life's myriad trials, when hopes wane,
Let not despair nor sorrow reign.
Be joyful, strong, in adversity's face,
For in cheer, life's challenges embrace.

Vedanta whispers, strength of mind is key,
For the weak-hearted, no victory shall be.
So, stand firm in faith, in goodness believe,
For in strength and love, divinity you'll retrieve.

In mankind today, a decline we see,
A loss of divine love, an increase in apathy.
Peace falters where Godly fear fades,
In human hearts, where darkness invades.

Hence, let love for God, morality's flame,
Fear of sin, guide our worldly game.
For Rama and Ravana, knowledge the same,
Yet their paths diverged, in life's grand game.

Ravana, in wisdom's misuse, a tragic fall,
Rama, in action and love, heeded life's call.
In welfare of all, his heart did rest,
In knowledge, virtue, he was the best.

So, let us walk the path Rama showed,
In love and goodness, let our lives be sowed.
In the rhythm divine, love is God's embrace,
A celestial dance, where spirits find their grace.

Begin with love, let it guide your day,
In love's embrace, let life's play sway.
For in love, to God, the path is laid,
In this journey of love, let life be made.

A Journey to Divinity

In the realm of human life, where desires weave,
Man suffers, his love in a narrow sheave.
For love, when constricted, loses its breath,
Its expansion is life, its contraction, death.

Behold, each soul, a divine spark aglow,
Children of God, in this worldly show.
Lord Krishna's words, in the Gita, resound,
In every being, the eternal Atma is found.

So widen your heart, embrace all as kin,
In unity and love, life's true journey begin.
For without broad feelings, humanity is blind,
In love's grand expanse, our true selves we find.

"See no evil, but the good in sight,
Hear no evil, in sounds of delight.
Talk no evil, but words of grace,
Think no evil, in thoughts embrace.

Do no evil, but acts that shine,
This is the path to the divine."
So simple the way, yet profound its reach,
In love and goodness, the soul's highest speech.

Why delve in rigors of spiritual quest,
When love's simple path offers eternal rest?
For not in austerity does divinity lie,
But in loving all, under God's watchful eye.

Moses, in love, shone with Jesus' light,
His face, a reflection of the divine sight.
And Ratnakara, once a robber so vile,
In Rama's name, found a life worthwhile.

Transformed, he became sage Valmiki, revered,
In his verses, Rama's radiance appeared.
For the giver and the composer, in essence, one,
As the Vedas proclaim, in wisdom's sun.

Know the good, and good you become,
In this truth, our spiritual journey is summed.
Think good, do good, in goodness abide,
In this way, true humanity is defined.

For a heart that harbors ill can never soar,
In the realms of divinity, forevermore.
So embrace love, let goodness be your guide,
In acts of compassion, let your spirit reside.

For in love and goodness, divinity is near,
In this simple truth, let your life steer.
Start with love, in love's embrace stay,
For this is the path, the divine way.

The Wisdom of Equanimity

In the grand tapestry of life, so vast and wide,
Human existence, a rare gem, in time's tide.
In rebirth-cycle, "human birth is rarest", it is said,
It's a culmination of past deeds, in this life's thread.

The essence of humanity, in 'manava' (human) lies,
"Not new," it whispers, beneath the skies.
In the tapestry of existence, echoes of the past unfold,
A boundless soul's odyssey, a story to be told.

Yet, in desires' grip, human often falls,
Forgetting his(/her) essence, in temptation's halls.
"Less luggage, more comfort," a sage's wise creed,
In simplicity, find life's truest need.

Life, a voyage long, through time's relentless sea,
Seek divinity in living, let that your beacon be.
Not a life of despair, but of divine light,
In happiness, find strength, in darkness, sight.

For trials will come, as sure as the dawn,
Yet like passing clouds, they'll be gone.
In difficulties, find not despair, but a chance to grow,
For in moral values, life's true colours show.

In Rama's tale, a lesson of virtue so bright,
Even in exile's shadow, he shone with light.
"Equanimity," he taught, in life's ebb and flow,
Pain and pleasure, victory and defeat, high and low.

A king by right, yet a wanderer by fate,
In his relinquishment, lessons so great.
For in adversity, courage he did find,
A poised, unshaken, in body and mind.

Hanuman, too, in Rama's reflection grew,
In contemplation, courage within him flew.
In Ravana's court, his valour did shine,
Yet, before Rama, humility's fine line.

For this is the wisdom, ancient and revered,
Be humble before the divine, courage against evil geared.
In life's dualities, find your balance and stand,
With humility and courage, hand in hand.

So tread this path, with a heart bold and meek,
In every challenge, life's wisdom seek.
For in this balance, your spirit will thrive,
In the eternal journey, truly alive.

Triumph Over Tempest

In the silent depths of the soul's dark night,
Lurk shadows of kama, krodha, lobha's blight.
Ravana, a tale of ruin, a dynasty lost,
In the fierce grip of desires, what a dreadful cost.

Annihilate these demons, of greed, desire, and rage,
For they are the foes that your heart must engage.
Not merely a story of ancient lore,
But a lesson profound, for evermore.

For desire, like a fire, consumes and burns,
And in the ashes of anger, no peace returns.
The greed, a chain, binds the soul in despair,
In its relentless grasp, life's joys are rare.

So heed this call, to control and contain,
The tumultuous passions, the inner disdain.
In this modern era, where excess reigns free,
A ceiling on desires, the true key to be.

The ruler may legislate, on land and wealth,
But the true dominion lies in the heart's stealth.
To master oneself, the greatest feat,
In the battle of wills, let not desires defeat.

For in the taming of these tempests wild,
Lies the path to peace, serene and mild.
Let not Ravana's fate, your destiny be,
In the chains of anger and desire, never free.

So rise above, with strength and grace,
In the mastery of self, find your rightful place.
For in the triumph over tempest's roar,
Lies the true victory, worth striving for.

Celestial Kinship:

In the epic tapestry of ancient lore,
Where heroes tread and legends soar,
Stands Ram, a figure of human grace,
Embracing all, transcending race.

His friendship with Sugreev, noble and grand,
And with Angada, prince of a distant land,
Hanuman, minister, loyal and wise,
In their bond, humanism's highest prize.

A kinship that crossed species' divide,
In Ram's heart, no prejudice did reside.
In kindness' ambassador, Rama stands tall,
Compassion's echo, embracing creatures, great and small.

In the realm of Ramayana, so old and revered,
A message of duty and ideology, clearly steered.
Expanding humanism, beyond mere human kin,
To embrace the divine, a new paradigm to begin.

No Alternative to Good Behavior, the tale resounds,
In Ram's victory, a profound truth abounds.
Against Ravan, power and talent amassed,
Yet, devoid of virtue, his fate was cast.

For in the battle of life, it's not might that reigns,
But good behavior, the ultimate chains.
The most gifted, in shadows may dwell,
If virtues abandoned, in morals they fell.

Ram, the epitome of righteousness and might,
Stood against wrong, for what's just and right.
A lesson eternal, in his saga we find,
Goodness and virtue, in them, true power aligned.

So let Ram's story, in our hearts reside,
A beacon of humanism, in which we take pride.
For in his journey, a truth so clear,
In goodness and love, let our paths steer.

The Timeless Ideal: Ram's Virtuous Saga

Valmiki's voice, through ages, rings,
Of Ram, the closest to virtue's springs.
In the Ramayana, his journey sings,
A life of trials, and ethical wings.

Through life's tempest, he walked so tall,
Maintaining ideals, amidst every fall.
In adversities' face, he stood like a wall,
A beacon of ethics, standing gall.

An ideal son, in love so deep,
A husband true, his vows to keep.
In ruling realms, his justice steep,
A brother kind, bonds to reap.

Even in war, his enemy found,
A divine adversary, honour bound.
Ram's story, in hearts, profound,
Beyond time, in its sacred mound.

Today's youth, in his tale, should delve,
A story of virtues, in their core to shelve.
Beyond religion, era, it does well,
In Ram's saga, life's truths swell.

Echoes of Eternity: Ramayana's Resonance:

In the ancient verses, a tale unfolds,
Ramayana's wisdom, in today's world it holds.
Amidst crises of values, crime's sinister dance,
A timeless guide, in its poetic expanse.

Moral compass shining, a radiant beam,
In the labyrinth of choices, a virtuous dream.
Resilience and hope, a triumphant song,
Rama's journey, in adversity, strong.

Relationships painted in hues of devotion,
Sita, Lakshmana, Hanuman's emotion.
In bonds, strength found in love's sweet embrace,
A reminder in chaos, of solace and grace.

Questioning minds, discernment's embrace,
Characters complex, virtues and flaws we trace.
Critical thinking spurred, norms to defy,
In the Ramayana's tapestry, truths lie.

No rulebook simplistic, life's nuanced dance,
Interpretations myriad, as we advance.
Engage with its wisdom, in varied hue,   A
guide to a life, righteous and true.

In conclusion, it's a framework, timeless and vast,
Not a quick fix, but a treasure amassed.
Hope, resilience, compassion it imparts,
A beacon of light in our searching hearts.

Remember, in its message, a world we can mold,
Drawing from its wisdom, in stories untold.
For a better tomorrow, in its embrace,
Ramayana's lessons, let us efface.

www.ingramcontent.com/pod-product-compliance
Lightning Source LLC
LaVergne TN
LVHW072336080526
838199LV00109B/435